Reconnection

Reconnection

Dualism to Holism in
Literary Study

Betty Jean Craige

The University of Georgia Press
Athens and London

© 1988 by the University of Georgia Press
Athens, Georgia 30602
All rights reserved
Set in Linotron 202 Times Roman with Helvetica Display.
The paper in this book meets the guidelines for permanence and
durability of the Committee on Production Guidelines for
Book Longevity of the Council on Library Resources.

Printed in the United States of America

92 91 90 89 88   5 4 3 2 1

Library of Congress Cataloging in Publication Data

Craige, Betty Jean.
  Reconnection: dualism to holism in literary
study.

  Bibliography: p.
  1. Literature—Philosophy—History. 2. Dualism.
3. Holism. 4. Humanities. 5. Interdisciplinary
approach to knowledge. I. Title.
PN45.C67 1988   801   87-16243
ISBN 0-8203-0987-7 (alk. paper)
ISBN 0-8203-1014-X (pbk.: alk. paper)

British Library Cataloging in Publication Data available

To the Lunch Group

Contents

Preface

Reconnection is a polemical book; it begins with an exploration of how literary study developed as an academic discipline during the period of Cartesian dualism and ends with an argument for a change in its practices. In order to present what I believe to be the discipline's main ideological assumptions, I am deliberately simplifying a very complex history, with the understanding that I shall probably offend by my degree of generalization specialists in various periods. I have written this book primarily to provide a discussion of our discipline's priorities, and I am open to ideas that others may have regarding the changes already under way in the academic structure of American higher education.

As *Reconnection* goes to press, a new book about American education has appeared: Allan Bloom's *The Closing of the American Mind*. *Reconnection* represents an alternative position to Bloom's regarding the function of the humanities in higher education.

Acknowledgments

I am indebted to many wonderful friends, from a variety of disciplines, who read, criticized, and offered suggestions for this book while I was writing it. I must thank first of all Jim Colvert, of the University of Georgia's English Department, for the enthusiastic support of the project he offered from its beginnings years ago, for all the long discussions that helped me formulate my ideas, and for the painstaking attention (philosophical and stylistic) he gave to every chapter. I owe much to Bernard Dauenhauer of Philosophy for both his encouragement and his thought-provoking questions and criticisms of the book; Bernie helped me to see the larger political context of my ideas, for which I am grateful. Gene Odum of Ecology inspired me to explore the implications for literary study of the ecological model and then encouraged me to use the word *holohumanities* (a word which not all of my friends like but one to which I am quite attached) to express the newer holistic discipline I see developing. And I thank Joel Black, Ron Bogue, and Egbert Krispyn of Comparative Literature, Carl Rapp and Anne Williams of English, and Glenda Thompson of Music, as well as Pat Perrin, now with the *Brain/Mind Bulletin,* Shari Benstock of the English Department at the University of Miami, and Bruce Franklin of the English Department at Rutgers University for their help with the entire manuscript; without their criticism I might not have had the confidence to range as widely as I have in telling the story of the discipline of literary study. Other dear friends have given much time and attention to individual chapters, for which I thank Sheila Bailey, Blue Calhoun, Lief Carter, Charles Doyle, Rosemary Franklin, Nelson Hilton, Lester Stephens, and Frank Warnke. And for helpful discussions, recommendations of pertinent books, and the location of references, I also thank Malcolm Call, Judith Cofer, Cameron Fincher, Stan Lindberg, Karen Orchard, Jean-Pierre Piriou, and Katja Wilson. Malcolm, who is Director of the University of Georgia Press, and Karen, Associate Director and Executive Editor, deserve special mention for their patience with my impatience, as does my editor, Ellen Harris.

I appreciate financial support from The University of Georgia Research Foundation.

I dedicate this book to my "Lunch Group," with whom—in the course of fourteen years' friendship—I began wondering how our profession acquired its present practices: to John Algeo, Sheila Bailey, Rodney Baine, Jim Colvert, Charlie Doyle, Coburn Freer, Bob Longshore, and Jane McWhorter. To absolve them of any guilt by association, however, I hasten to say that we frequently disagree!

Reconnection

Introduction

The old idea that knowledge is power is now obsolete. To achieve power today
you need knowledge about knowledge.

—Alvin Toffler, *Previews and Premises*

Instead of "knowledge," let's say "understanding."

—Eugene Odum

Perhaps the reason that humanists have begun to examine the premises of
our various disciplines is that the age of the discipline is ending.

In *Reconnection* I shall investigate the discipline of literary study in relation
to Cartesian dualism, which provided for the objectification of knowledge and,
consequently, academic specialization in a body of knowledge. Although my
major interest is the discipline's present function in American society, I shall
trace its development from the time of the Scientific Revolution, with the
hypothesis that literature and the discipline of literary study obtained definition in opposition to science and, later, in opposition to other apparently utilitarian endeavors. I wish to show how the emergence of the holistic paradigm
means an increase in interdisciplinary, or nondisciplinary, research and teaching in the humanities and a shift in focus from canonized texts to methods of
contextual interpretation, a shift that is occurring now.

To tell the story I have chosen to explore the impact upon the profession of
a few profound, culture-wide ideas, articulated by thinkers engaged in a variety of intellectual endeavors—such thinkers as René Descartes, Francis Bacon, Percy Bysshe Shelley, Matthew Arnold, Charles Darwin, Charles
William Eliot, Werner Heisenberg, T. S. Eliot, Virginia Woolf, the New
Critics, J. Hillis Miller, Eugene Odum, and Jacques Derrida—whom I shall
treat as representatives of these ideas. I must unfortunately exclude the writings of many other figures pertinent to this study, because my purpose is not
to give a detailed history of the discipline's establishment in the academy but

instead to illuminate certain forces shaping the profession. And since I begin the story in the seventeenth century and end with the late 1980s, I shall be deliberately simplifying a complex sequence of events in order to disclose a pattern.

I expect that many literary scholars will not believe that the discipline as we have known it in the twentieth century is changing fundamentally. And those scholars will reject my argument that the reorientation from a canon of great literary works, once the discipline's objectified subject matter, toward the discourse that has constituted that canon, with a new attention to ways of understanding, will save the humanities. To scholars believing that the aim of the discipline is and should be to acquaint individual students with "the best which has been thought and said in the world" (Arnold, *Complete Works* 10: 56), such a reorientation appears as a loss of traditional values, a lack of appreciation for the aesthetic, a chaos in which barbaric left-wingers criticize literary geniuses for sexism and racism. I believe, however, that only by radically changing our teaching and research practices to focus on the social construction of our knowledge, of our "literary" expression, and to study ways of interpreting texts (of whatever kind) *contextually* can we reintegrate the discipline into our society's intellectual-political life.

In this century we have seen various technological revolutions in which the humanities participated only in opposition. Society left to the specialists the problems issuing from atomic energy and chemical control of insects, ignoring any insights humanists might have offered into the effect of the new technology on the environment, on society, and on humankind's future. Now we are in the midst of another technological revolution—of which biotechnology is one aspect—and if we humanists are disturbed by the ethical questions raised by *in vitro* fertilization, organ transplanting, genetic engineering, and the competition among universities for commercial grants, for example, then we must involve ourselves actively in thinking and writing about these matters. For our society will need thinkers capable of understanding the implications of words and actions to interpret the rapid changes in our increasingly technological state. In the discipline of literary study, our attention to literature for its aesthetic expression alone has disengaged us from some major social issues. By recognizing that, and by reorienting our attention toward modes of interpreting texts in general, we may recover the position of centrality that the humanities once enjoyed. In so doing we shall transform the discipline of literary study into a new (holistic) "holohumanities," without boundaries, which will define itself not in opposition to the sciences but rather in cooperation, and which will speak not solely to other academics but to the public as well.

Holohumanities is a word yet to be found in a dictionary, a word therefore odious to many humanists who take pride in the use of language and who dislike the influx of words contrived to rarefy concepts expressible in good English. I suggest that we consider using that word, however, because the word "humanities" has implied, in the past three hundred years, an isolation from science, technology, and politics.

The university has traditionally served society by preserving and advancing knowledge, to which end it has maintained—in theory—a distance from the immediate political concerns of its culture, a distance that has served as the basis of academic freedom. Within its own walls it has divided knowledge into disciplines, reflecting the specialization that has dominated our culture for the past hundred years, and its scholars contribute to society by teaching and doing research within disciplines. Both scientists and humanists specialize to extend the frontiers of knowledge, and we are rewarded for expertise in our chosen fields.

Yet the very distance that scholars have demanded from politics to pursue knowledge in occasionally unpopular ways has created the illusion for many people that academic concerns are irrelevant to the purposes of "the real world." The remark "That's academic!" often means "That's irrelevant!" The Supplement to the *Oxford English Dictionary* gives as a definition of *academic*: "Not leading to a decision; unpractical; theoretical, formal, or conventional"; in art, "Conforming too rigidly to the principles of an academy; excessively formal." To scholars, *academic* is an adjective of approbation, meaning "disciplinary," as in academic literary criticism or academic art criticism, criticism that is directed toward scholars in the discipline and that follows the conventions of scholarly writing; it is also a noun denoting a person who teaches and studies in a department of a college or a university, and who wins tenure and promotion by doing disciplinary research judged valuable by his or her peers in the discipline. But to nonscholars, an academic is an inhabitant of the "ivory tower," by which they mean a refuge from the social issues of the day.

How did the perception of irrelevance come about? How have the humanities—particularly literary study—served Western culture? How did its scholars come to develop the particular teaching and research practices that now characterize the profession? Why is literary study considered worthy of inclusion in the academic curriculum? As the culture shifts from the industrial age into the information age, from Cartesian dualism into holism, what will be the function of the humanities? What will be the relationship of the university to the society that supports it? These are the questions that have motivated the writing of this book.

Specialization in a body of knowledge is an aspect of, or an effect of, the paradigm of Cartesian dualism governing our culture since the Scientific Revolution, which took place between 1500 and 1700, when Western civilization gained confidence in knowledge obtainable by "objective" observation of nature. According to Marshall McLuhan, Walter Ong, and other recent scholars of the effects of writing on a culture, the dualism that we call Cartesian resulted in part from print literacy: to them, René Descartes' early-seventeenth-century idea that reality was divided between self and world, between spirit and matter, between mind and body, was made possible by the printing press, invented around 1450, which objectified knowledge in the printed text and thereby brought about a change in human consciousness in the expanded reading public. The reader of the text became the "impartial" observer of the world, and language (made manifest in print) served as the apparently neutral medium of description. The philosophical distance from "reality" given by print literacy allowed Francis Bacon to develop his Inductive Method of investigation—collecting data by observation, developing a hypothesis, and then testing the hypothesis by further observation—and Descartes to conceive of reality as *res extensa*, the "extended thing," external to the observer.

A paradigm—the model by which a culture constructs reality—moves into place as the effect of multitudinous forces: scientific, political, social, economic, and religious. Print, effecting a culture-wide literacy, spread the ideas of Protestantism and democracy across Europe; print helped bring about Cartesian dualism and scientific empiricism; print gave the middle classes new forms of entertainment; print made possible the newspaper and the novel. And print secularized the culture, releasing readers from dependence upon external authorities, such as the Church, for knowledge about the world, by enabling readers to gain such knowledge on their own and to think for themselves. The growth of science became an index to the rate of secularization. The dualist paradigm was supported, however, not only by the growing print literacy and the scientific discoveries of the period but also by social and economic events. The Industrial Revolution, occurring in England between 1750 and 1850, reinforced in the mind of the populace the subordination of nature to human control that Bacon had announced; and its establishment of a proletariat increased awareness among the intelligentsia of the difference between intellectual and manual labor and of the preferability of intellectual—and, by implication, apparently nonutilitarian—activity, which as an index of social class and leisure time carried prestige. By contributing to the filth and the poverty of the cities, industrialism seemed to verify Descartes' distinction of spirit and matter, or self and world, influencing the Romantic desire for transcendence over an unattractive material reality.

Modern science began, according to many historians, in the seventeenth century, when various intellectuals interested in understanding nature attempted to throw off medieval superstitions and the dictatorial power of the Church. Reacting against the synthesizing character of medieval Christianity's explanations of the universe, the new scientists sought to analyze sensory reality with a degree of certainty that was empirical rather than religious. To this end Bacon reoriented science from medieval scholasticism, the wisdom of individuals, to a collaborative enterprise of specialists which included the "mechanical arts" and which thereby contributed to the culture's material welfare, reversing previous notions of science and art (Rossi 174–175). Science after Bacon included technology and had for its purpose the transformation of society. The arts, or rather the humanities, took up the field of learning that science had abandoned: philosophy, as well as history, the study of ancient Greek and Roman writers, and eventually the study of "literature."

In the Middle Ages the "liberal arts," born of the old distinction between the intellectual work of free men and the physical work of slaves, which had become the distinction between rational knowledge and practical knowledge, had included logic, rhetoric, grammar, arithmetic, geometry, astronomy, and music. The "mechanical arts," formulated in the twelfth century, included the making of clothing, the making of tools and shelter, agriculture, hunting, navigation, medicine, and theater, with architecture, sculpture, and painting subsumed under *armatura*, the making of tools and shelter. In this system poetry belonged with logic, rhetoric, and grammar (Kristeller 507–8). Not until the sixteenth century in Italy, when Vasari separated painting, sculpture, and architecture from the crafts (Kristeller 514), did the fine arts exist as a concept. The Quarrel Between the Ancients and the Moderns, which began in the last quarter of the seventeenth century, produced a reorganization of learning by distinguishing between the disciplines that depended upon individual talent and taste and those that depended upon mathematics and the accumulation of knowledge (Kristeller 525). This distinction, to which Bacon had contributed by rejecting the ancients as authorities on nature, became the basis for our modern opposition of the arts and humanities to the sciences. In the dualist paradigm, in which the spirit/matter opposition took over the ancient distinction between "liberal" and "mechanical," the arts and humanities concerned themselves with a subjective spiritual reality and the sciences with an objective material reality.

Descartes's division of reality into *res cogitans* and *res extensa* revealed the culture's interest not only in the objectified world, *res extensa*, but also in the self, for his philosophy issued from his fundamental certainty in the existence of the rational subject: "I think, therefore I am." The discourse that we now call literature, which from the eighteenth century has been defined as a category of imaginative writing, served to express the human emotions and values that science and industry ignored. As writing that gave not an empirically verifiable truth about an external reality but rather a subjective truth, literature was distinguished from both science and history; and as writing that supposedly had no utilitarian purpose, literature was distinguished from laws, treaties, and technical writing. In the search for absolute Truth literature claimed superiority to science and history, because literature, according to its advocates, expressed knowledge of the soul, whereas science and history disclosed only material facts.[1]

Just as it had obtained its definition, the discipline of literary study obtained its place in the academic curriculum in relation to science. In America science did not become a discipline with a home in the university until after the publication of Charles Darwin's *On the Origin of Species* in 1859. For science had to overcome the centuries-old assumption that the proper studies for educated men were the liberal arts, which did not include Baconian science, and it had to overcome the objection of the theologians on the colleges' governing boards that science would convert America's youth to atheism. Darwinian science questioned not only religious views of creation but also the static conception of knowledge—that knowledge was a fixed body of truth—and consequently the traditional function of education, which was to transmit that knowledge into the minds of students (Hofstadter 14). The scientific goal of continuous inquiry into the nature of things and the scientific method of testing hypotheses did not accord with the ideals of the liberal arts colleges: science's challenge to the curriculum was a challenge to the very notion of knowledge that governed education in the nineteenth century.

Thus the debate on reforming the college curriculum waged in such journals as *Popular Science Monthly* presented a choice of two modes of learning, two modes of apprehending reality. Advocates of science in America argued the superiority of science over disciplines that could not produce exact knowledge, reinforcing for the academy the dichotomy of science and the humanities. Chauncey Wright wrote in 1877 that science would finally be objective "when it ceases to be associated with our fears, our respects, our aspirations—our emotional nature; when it ceases to prompt questions as to what relates to our personal destiny, our ambitions, our moral worth; when it ceases to have man, his personal and social nature, as its central and controlling objects" (49).

This left the humanists, many of whom found Wright's values repugnant, with the realm of the subjective. In part because of the pressure from scientists to institute the (useful) study of French and German in the universities, in part because of the pressure from the utilitarians to teach modern literature in addition to Greek and Latin, in part because of the new interest in "the mother-tongue," and in part because of their own belief that literature expressed man's soul, humanists made the study of modern literature a university discipline. As religion declined in importance in the post–Civil War curriculum, literature accompanied "moral philosophy" in prompting questions regarding human destiny, ambitions, and moral worth.

The professors of literature in the 1870s and 1880s sought to distinguish their aims from those of the scientists, yet they gradually accepted the scientists' model for research, establishing specialization in an area of literature and publication of research as requisite to the academic success of literary scholars. Literary study thus became a graduate discipline. Having evolved from the study of rhetoric and grammar when literature became objectified into a definable category of writing, the new discipline justified its right to award a Ph.D. by defining a field for research: philology. With research becoming a major function of all institutions offering graduate education, even many humanists came to assume that the means to gain knowledge of the world was to examine a small enough portion of it to obtain empirical validity when making statements about it.

In the early twentieth century, in rebellion against philological and historical research, the "New Critics" turned their attention to the literary work itself as a "verbal icon." With the goal of acquainting students with literature's "poetic" aspects and "universal" values, these theorists developed new textbook anthologies, whose effect upon the profession was to make the canon the primary subject matter for the discipline and literary interpretation its main activity. Although the New Critics continued to argue the superiority of the humanities over the sciences, they were actually following the scientists' reductionist pattern of isolating events and entities for objective scrutiny, extracting texts from contexts. "Scientific" had come to mean "objective," and objectivity marked good scholarship.

In the dualist paradigm between the Renaissance and the twentieth century, science had increasingly challenged the claims of religion to explain the world, the claims of the soul to operate independently of physical forces, and the claims of literature to give the higher truth. By the end of the nineteenth century, however, science itself was undoing the paradigm that had supported it, the belief in objectivity. The breakdown in the subject/object model would mean the end of the oppositions of spirit/matter, mind/body, self/world, and—eventually—literature/science. Generally speaking, Cartesian dualism, which assumed the mind's independence of both body and "external reality," governed in natural history (which became biology) until the middle of the nineteenth century, in art until the late nineteenth century, in physics until the early twentieth century, in medicine until the mid-twentieth century, and in the methods and structure of higher education through the present.

The belief in the theological distinction between soul and body, which implied a distinction between mankind and animals, was threatened by Darwinian natural selection in 1859. The belief in the possibility of objective representation, implicit in the realist painting of fixed perspective, was first challenged by Impressionism and Post-Impressionism in the 1870s and 1880s and then undermined completely by cubism in the first decade of the twentieth century. Newtonian physics, in which time and space were absolute, gave way to relativity and quantum mechanics between 1905, the year of Einstein's Special Theory of Relativity, and 1927, the year of Heisenberg's Indeterminacy Principle. The belief in the mind/body separation that had dominated Western medicine weakened with the introduction of phenothiazines, tranquilizers used therapeutically to alleviate schizophrenia, in the 1950s. And in higher education the boundaries between the intellectual disciplines established in the late nineteenth century are being questioned now, as is the concept of the discipline itself; yet our departmental structure, our promotion procedures, and our teaching and research practices for the most part imply the dualist paradigm.

From Einstein the culture learned that one had to take into account point of view when describing phenomena, and from Heisenberg that any investigation of phenomena must include consideration of our means of investigation, that our methods determine the nature of our discoveries—in short, that we are involved in what we see. Heisenberg and others elaborated the philosophical implications of his Indeterminacy Principle to show that all discourse, whether humanistic or scientific, carried the values and interests of its culture, that no event or text had intrinsic meaning, and that no event or text was definable independently of context, which always included the perceiver. Now both history and science are discussed in terms of the values and interests implicit in points of view; now humanists and scientists, aware that investigator and world cannot be separated, have discovered mutual concerns. In the late twentieth century literary theorists, no longer believing literature to be intrinsically distinct from other discourses, are looking to science for an understanding of how our culture makes order. And a few scientists, no longer believing science to be absolutely objective, are looking to the humanities for an understanding of our culture's values, values that determine the directions science takes.

The new relativism in these disciplines has come not only from art and physics but also from politics: the national political upheaval of the sixties. The civil rights movement and the Vietnam War created a generation of young people skeptical of the corporate state, whose model of specialization discouraged a philosophical appraisal of our national goals by citizens who were not part of the government or of the military. Moreover, the government tended to recognize as legitimate only that criticism rendered by specialists. But to those opposed to the United States' involvement in Southeast Asia, for example, the information provided by the military or political specialists seemed to carry the values of their interested viewpoints, the values those specialists had absorbed in the course of their training. The difficulty of national self-reflection appeared integral to the culture's social structure, for the complexity of the modern technological world required specialists in myriad fields for the welfare of society; modern science could not advance without highly trained specialists. Yet the humanities, which might have produced the needed cross-disciplinary thinkers to analyze events in the context of the whole political-social-economic system, had been shaped in the academy by scientific reductionism, and most of its scholars were specialists as well, specialists in areas of literature or history, limited by the range of their expertise.

Many Vietnam-era thinkers identified as a problem the traditionally lauded independence of the university from political issues. The idealized separation of scholar from society that was justified by the long-held distinction between "liberal" knowledge and utilitarian concerns had found a practical purpose in the late nineteenth-century controversy over Darwinian biology in American universities. Our notion of academic freedom, adopted from German universities during those decades to protect both students and professors from social pressures, particularly pressure from religious groups, was based on the belief that the pursuit of truth required an independence of politics, that because "truth" was occasionally unpopular it should be protected from a perhaps hostile society. The freedom from social pressures implied as well, however, the scholar's withdrawal from political debate. In its assumption that the university benefited society most by shunning any engagement in political issues, the academy had reduced not only the scientist's responsibilities to the pursuit of apparently "nonpolitical" truth but the humanist's as well, in effect restricting scholars (ideally) to the pursuit of "nonpolitical" disciplinary knowledge—"pure" knowledge, which defined itself as "nonutilitarian." Yet in the Vietnam period scientists held contracts from the government and from industry for military and technological research.

In the sixties many intellectuals, having come to distrust the media and the government, learned from practical experience that information carried ideology, that there was no "pure" knowledge. "Truth" seemed inseparable from context, which included both speaker and listener, both author and reader. Becoming suspicious as well of the knowledge presented by the established intellectual disciplines and of the established modes of disciplinary research, they interrogated various apparent boundaries—the boundary between the university and society, the boundaries between disciplines, the boundaries between kinds of writing—for those boundaries obstructed the cultural self-reflection that radicals believed was crucial to the health of the country. Radicals became relativists, aware that the point of view determined the view.

In the climate of skepticism the discipline of literary study underwent a radical critique as well. The dualist assumption made by Hiram Corson of Cornell in 1910 that "spiritual consciousness is certainly a more vital kind of knowledge than any we can have of material things" (Corson 21–22) continued to support the separation of literary texts from other kinds of texts and the separation of literary study from history and sociology; and although this philosophical foundation was hardly explicit in the writings of the scholars, it functioned to justify the study of literature as an intellectual discipline. The goal of close textual analysis of individual literary works, proposed by the New Critics in the late 1930s and 1940s, still dominated the practice of professors in the 1960s.

In the decade of the sixties, many young people, eager to obtain the intellectual skills requisite to thoughtful analysis of cultural problems, chose to obtain graduate degrees in literature, in the belief that the study of literature would encompass history, philosophy, politics, aesthetics, and linguistics, and would thus offer the opportunity to see the interrelatedness of humankind's endeavors. But after a few years in the profession, some became impatient with the specialization required by the discipline and impatient with the assumption that literature was generally nonpolitical: if literature was considered above politics, above "material things," then its scholars were politically divorced from society. To a politicized generation the discipline of literary study, by devoting itself to finding "higher" truths and by encouraging specialization in an area of literature, had rendered itself incapable of addressing particular social problems. The question arose: Did the disciplinary system itself, as it operated in graduate studies in literature and in the departmental structure of higher education, inhibit the development of wide-ranging thinkers?

To what extent the frustration of the Vietnam generation influenced the recent critique of the discipline's ideology is of course highly debatable: I wish here only to suggest a way of making sense out of major changes taking place in the profession now. In the seventies, many postwar scholars brought to the academy a habit of making ideological connections between events. No longer believers in "objectivity," we began to see connections between Cartesian dualism and cultural imperialism, between dualism and the belief in a nonpolitical science, between dualism and patriarchy, between dualism and racism, between dualism and the white, male literary canon, between dualism and literature as a category of text. Following Heisenberg, we shifted attention from any so-called "external" order of things to the culture's process of making that order. Scholars took on the project of questioning the "truths" of the disciplines, to reveal their presuppositions, their cultural specificity, their political interests; the various liberation groups—Women's Liberation, Black Liberation, Gay Liberation—set about rewriting the nation's history, disregarding disciplinary boundaries, to reveal the ideology hidden behind the accepted versions of our culture's past.[2] Feminist scientists began investigating the hidden ideology of empirical science. Theorists of the humanities, the social sciences, and the physical sciences joined each other to form the new metadiscipline of "Theory," whose function was to criticize the ideologies of the disciplines. Finally, some have undermined even Theory, acknowledging that no discourse is value-free, not even their own.

This analysis of our society's values generated an impatience with vertical social hierarchies. Western culture's privileging of man over woman, of white over black, had left its trace in the organization of family, community, labor, government, and university. And the disclosure of structural injustices required a critique of all social institutions—across disciplinary lines. Nothing was considered sacred; nothing was immune to social critique. Now intellectuals in all fields are recognizing the need for thinkers to range outside traditional disciplines to ponder the directions our technological knowledge is taking us. Asking questions about the traditional relationship of the university to the society it serves, the disciplinary nature of the culture's search for knowledge, the origins of the disciplines, and the structure of academic administration, intellectuals have become increasingly critical of the model of specialization according to which the function of scholars is to teach and to do research within disciplines.

If no knowledge is value-free, then what are the implications to the supposition, still held by many, that universities do nonpolitical research? What is the political relationship of the university to the culture that supports it? How will humanists do wide-ranging critical thinking in a university environment in which we are rewarded primarily for being specialists in an area of literature or history? Does the present structure of the academy restrict the intellectual's responsibility in a free society to criticize the culture's social institutions?

These questions are being asked today by the new generation of academics. Alvin Toffler, in *The Third Wave*, has written that

Today . . . we stand on the edge of a new age of synthesis. In all intellectual fields, from the hard sciences to sociology, psychology, and economics—especially economics—we are likely to see a return to large-scale thinking, to general theory, to the putting of the pieces back together again. For it is beginning to dawn on us that our obsessive emphasis on quantified detail without context, on progressively finer and finer measurement of smaller and smaller problems, leaves us knowing more and more about less and less. (130)

According to Toffler, who follows Dewey, Heisenberg, McLuhan, and others, Cartesian dualism has run its course. Everywhere the mechanistic subject/object model in which, according to Bacon, man's purpose was to dominate nature, is giving way to an interactive, holistic, ecological model. In the academy, the institutionalization of the holistic paradigm is about to transform the disciplines, the methods and purposes of research, the practices of the academic profession, and even the structure of knowledge. The culture-wide reorientation will, of course, ultimately express itself in a new relationship between the academy and society. Ideally, in such a future, the public will no longer use the phrase "That's academic" to mean "That's irrelevant."

1

Dualism and the
Concept of Literature

It was as if print, uniform and repeatable commodity that it was, had the power of creating a new hypnotic superstition of the book as independent of and uncontaminated by human agency.

—Marshall McLuhan, *The Gutenberg Galaxy*

In this new world, the book was less like an utterance, and more like a thing.

—Walter J. Ong, *Orality and Literacy*

McLuhan and Ong, both scholars of English literature, have called our attention to the cultural transformation of consciousness that occurred with the spread of print literacy in Europe following the mid-fifteenth-century invention of the printing press (McLuhan, *Gutenberg Galaxy*, *Understanding Media*, *Medium Is Massage*; Ong, *Orality and Literacy*).[1] In their argument, the reader's relationship with the printed page reproduced itself in the individual's relationship with reality, which now seemed distanced from the individual in the same way that the text was distanced from the reader. The process of reading to obtain knowledge oriented the reader toward vision as the major sense on which to rely for an understanding of reality and consequently separated the individual from the object of vision, the world. Through an immensely complex evolutionary process, the reader/text separation became, in the consciousness of the newly print-literate population, the self/world separation.

The advent of print literacy contributed to a shift in paradigm from the medieval wholeness of self-in-world to self/world dualism in changing the cognitive relationship of human beings to their environment. In the Middle Ages the reading of manuscripts did not foster the illusion that the information in them was "independent of and uncontaminated by human agency." Medieval manuscripts presented their statements about the world, to those who could read them, in the handwriting of the copiers, and the statements gained their authority by their relation to the Bible or to such canonical thinkers as Aristotle and Saint Augustine. The vast majority of the population of Europe through the fifteenth century, unable to read the manuscripts, depended on the Church scholars for their religious knowledge. Obtaining information aurally, by listening to priests and to each other, illiterate people (according to Ong) were not inclined to dissociate utterances about the world from the situations in which they heard the utterances. Their knowledge of sacred matters came from the men of the Church, whom they knew, and their knowledge of secular matters came from their friends and from personal experiences.

Print, however, by appearing to represent a reality external to any single knower, established a context-free discourse (Ong 78). The identically reproducible printed text, which itself carried no physical mark of its author's personality, and which was occasionally accompanied by identically reproducible drawings (woodcuts, engravings, etchings), seemed to re-present the world objectively, depicting the same "reality" for every reader, a reality in which the reader did not participate. Moreover, because print looked like a neutral medium for communication, giving no indication in its appearance of its information content, print made language seem a neutral medium for the communication of observations. By separating information from its context— that is, by "containing" it on the printed page—print also provided for the reader the illusion that reality, like that information, was divisible into parts and external to the reader. Within two centuries of the invention of print, as the culture internalized print literacy, the order the printed text gave to the world had become the order the culture believed was intrinsic to the world and separate from the observer. Print thus promoted the Cartesian assumptions that reality was definable independently of any single perceiver; that, accordingly, the perceiver was definable independently of the external reality; that the perceiver could examine reality objectively, in its various parts; and that language was a neutral medium for the recording of objective data.

Furthermore, insofar as it turned the culture's attention outward to a reality whose apparent order did not include the perceiver, print literacy turned the individual's attention inward to the apparently autonomous self. For oral culture the major source of information was the social world, and the knowledgeable individual was a part of that social world; but for print culture the major source of information was the text, and the knowledgeable individual was not a part of the text. The reading of printed texts, which was increasingly done in private and in silence, contributed to this self-consciousness, not only by isolating the reader but also by giving the reader greater opportunity for self-reflection. Both world, as given by the text, and self, as excluded from the text, became "things," subject to analysis. Print thus isolated information as discrete bits of "truth" about the world, isolated the reader from the world of the text, even from the community, and established vision as the primary means for the individual to obtain information.

The separation of self from world effected by print literacy made for scientific empiricism. In contributing to the objectification of reality, print encouraged secular investigation of nature, helping to bring about the Scientific Revolution. In exposing the literate populace to a world far vaster than the illiterate could have been able to comprehend, and in making available multiple copies of such texts as the Bible, print encouraged individual thought about the world and about God, thus helping to bring about the Protestant Reformation. In making vision the primary means to obtain information about reality, print influenced the aesthetic of realism in the arts. By the end of the seventeenth century the culture-wide dualism manifested itself in Newtonian science, representational painting of fixed perspective, and the novel, which to varying degrees depended for their form on the notion that the self (the scientist, the painter, the author) could observe the world impartially, from a point of view outside events.

Descartes, in the late 1630s and early 1640s, mapped out the philosophical implications of the spirit/matter dualism that print had helped to bring about and that had come to characterize intellectual work in Europe. Putting everything into doubt but his own subjectivity, Descartes developed a proof of the existence of both self and an external material reality. His *Discourse on the Method* set up rules of procedure toward knowledge: (1) never to accept anything as true without evidence; (2) to divide each problem into as many parts as necessary for a solution; (3) to direct thoughts in an orderly fashion, beginning with the simplest objects and ascending to the more complex; and (4) to make enumerations and general surveys to leave nothing out (20–21). In the *Meditations* he distinguished between *res cogitans* (thinking thing) and *res extensa* (extended thing), making both mind and world into "things," and then connected the mind, or the soul, with God, whose existence he inferred as the Creator of himself and of everything else. He included his own body in *res extensa*, because, unlike the mind, it was divisible (121).

Descartes articulated philosophically the emerging paradigm in which nature was an object for secular study. The proposition that the world was distinct from the mind, divisible, and therefore capable of being examined in parts (an operating assumption for Bacon several decades before Descartes), came out of the medieval spirit/matter dualism that itself can be traced back to Plato. The reification of phenomena, whether reality, events, or the mind itself, made possible the quantification of phenomena, which in turn seemed to give scientific legitimacy to ranking, already in the Western culture as the Great Chain of Being (Gould, *Mismeasure* 24). The division of phenomena into discrete entities, with the ordering of those entities according to increasing complexity, appears in the division of knowledge into disciplines, the practice of specialization, the hierarchical ordering of texts, and even the twentieth-century academic practice of the objectification and quantification of research. Combined with the spirit/matter (soul/body, self/world) dualism, the hierarchical ordering of phenomena yielded a means for the culture to evaluate everything in terms of "higher" and "lower."

The new respect for the natural world as the source of knowledge was accompanied by new attitudes toward writing and toward the author. In *The Great Instauration* (1620) Bacon had rejected the ancients as sources of information on nature and had rejected the rhetorical style of the ancients as appropriate language for the description of nature:

> First then, away with antiquities, and citations or testimonies of authors; also with disputes and controversies and differing opinions; everything in short which is philological. Never cite an author except in a matter of doubtful credit: never introduce a controversy unless in a matter of great moment. And for all that concerns ornaments of speech, similitudes, treasury of eloquence, and such like emptinesses, let it be utterly dismissed. Also let all those things which are admitted be themselves set down briefly and concisely, so that they may be nothing less than words. For no man who is collecting and storing up materials for ship-building or the like, thinks of arranging them elegantly, as in a shop, and displaying them so as to please the eye; all his care is that they be sound and good, and that they be so arranged as to take up as little room as possible in the warehouse. And this is exactly what should be done here. (4: 254–55)

In demanding a nonrhetorical writing for the description of nature, Bacon was instrumental in formulating the distinction between poetic language and ordinary language that came to underlie the distinction between literature and such other discourses as history and science, as well as the distinction within literature between poetry and prose. By implying that language was potentially a neutral medium to communicate information, Bacon separated content from form, privileging content: he separated the message from the medium. For this scientist, nonrhetorical language, like printed prose, had no suasive power in itself. Rhetorical language, on the other hand, did; its form, designed to arouse the emotions of the reader, or listener, hid its content, its message, in a "treasury of eloquence" (which literary scholars would later interpret). And poetry on the printed page did in fact call attention to itself as a visible medium. Behind all Bacon's assumptions was the dualism Descartes was to expound: that spirit was separate from matter and that self was separate from world. Bacon associated rhetorical language with expression of the spirit and nonrhetorical language with description of the world.

Bacon was not alone in discriminating rhetorical from nonrhetorical language, but he was, by virtue of the breadth of his essays, one of the most influential thinkers of the late Renaissance for both the humanities and the sciences. Through his association of "ornaments of speech, similitudes, treasury of eloquence, and such like emptinesses" with the practice of citing the ancients, whom he refused to accept as authorities on nature, Bacon set up the opposition between the humanities, which from the Renaissance had been concerned with Greek and Latin texts, and the sciences, an opposition that turned into the late-seventeenth-century Quarrel Between the Ancients and the Moderns. However, Bacon did not trivialize poesy (by which he meant "feigned history") intentionally; indeed he praised it for expressing the spiritual condition of humanity, for presenting a "more perfect order" than one could find in nature "since the fall": "So that this Poesy conduces not only to delight but also to magnanimity and morality. Whence it may be fairly thought to partake somewhat of a divine nature; because it raises the mind and carries it aloft, accommodating the shows of things to the desires of the mind, not (like reason and history) buckling and bowing down the mind to the nature of things" (4: 316).

In this passage, where he declared poesy capable not only of delighting but also of improving the soul, thus leading to "magnanimity and morality," Bacon gave an early defense of literature.[2] Because literature could present a "more perfect order" than could history, which recounted events of a fallen world, literature could inspire readers to lead better lives. And if "true history" of the fallen, material world wearied the mind, then "feigned history" could refresh it, serving the reader as spiritual nourishment. Bacon was appropriating for his Christian age Aristotle's argument that poetry was "higher" and more philosophical than history, because poetry expressed the universal and history the particular (35). For Bacon the universal was the divine.

In *Of the Dignity and Advancement of Learning* Bacon had indirectly presented a rationale for literary study: to disclose the moral message—the connection with the divine—hidden in the rhetorical language of poesy. And the defining of poesy as imaginative writing whose language contained valuable secrets went hand in hand with the rise of a profession devoted to disclosing those secrets: in short the establishment of the category of "feigned history" meant the establishment of the practice of literary interpretation. The increasingly secular culture had come to treat secular imaginative works in the way the Middle Ages had treated religious texts: giving them value by interpreting them. And the individual supposedly profited similarly—through moral improvement.

In making distinctions between the imagination and nature, between poesy and science, and between poesy and history, Bacon anticipated literary scholars' later privileging of imaginative texts over texts that served the more practical function of representing accurately actual events. Yet by defining science as an institution serving the material needs of mankind, Bacon ultimately encouraged consideration of literature as extraneous to society's purposes and inspired the later battle between the liberal arts and utilitarian learning. After Bacon, poetry was defended against the charge that it was useless to society in comparison with science, that it was mere entertainment ("ornaments of speech"), by arguments that it gave human beings a spiritual knowledge that science did not. Yet in the secularization of the culture, as intellectuals lost their belief in God, and as poetry consequently lost its presumed connection with divinity, poetry—that is, literature—was defended as the expression of human subjectivity or as the expression of individual reality. By the late twentieth century, as thinkers began considering the self to be socially constructed, literature appeared more and more to be mere entertainment.

Thus with his opposition of the two kinds of writing, reflecting the subjective and objective realities respectively, Bacon had unwittingly marginalized the rhetorical. Nietzsche's announcement of the death of God in 1882 was for literary study a premature announcement of its own decline—as a definable discipline with definable subject matter—a hundred years later, for the belief in God, which was a belief in a spiritual reality independent of the material, had justified literary study as an intellectual discipline.

As Michel Foucault has argued (125–26), in the Middle Ages the truthfulness of what we would now call a scientific assertion (a statement regarding medicine or cosmology, for example) depended on its attachment to its author, but by the seventeenth century the truthfulness of such an assertion could be verified by reference to nature, for nature had become a legitimate object of study. No longer serving to validate the scientific text, the author's name signified only the author's role in developing the theory. Yet from the seventeenth century on, in the discourse that we now call literary, the author's name did indeed validate the text, determining for the reader its source. In other words, the discourse requiring authority was now the literary, rather than the scientific. This interest in the "literary" author arose in part because the subject/object dualism dictated an opposition between texts which told an empirical truth, as did history and science, and texts which did not. The latter, once print literacy had made the culture "self" conscious, were generally considered to issue from the imagination of individual authors.

The perceived autonomy of a literary work, now "less like an utterance and more like a thing," combined with the new capitalist concept of property, led to the copyright, which an oral culture could not have understood. In an oral culture an utterance "belonged" only briefly to the speaker, who would not have thought to claim originality for it, since the speaker was participating in a social situation, responding to other utterances, presenting ideas that were to a large extent those of the community. When print reified ideas, by containing them on the printed page, and separated them from their authors, those ideas became products of labor and therefore subject to possession. But whose? Indicative of the slowness with which the culture granted the status of originator to the author was the nature of the early copyright laws: the sixteenth-century laws benefited not the author but the publisher, who paid the author but received the exclusive rights to a text himself (probably because not until the eighteenth century could the publisher generate enough income from a book to support both himself and the author). In 1710, in England, new copyright laws recognized the author as the originator of the text: a statute of Anne shifted protection from the publisher to the author, whose work it protected for twenty-eight years, and thereby gave monetary value to the author's words.

The Cartesian subject/object dualism which at first characterized the capitalist relationship of publishers to their products came to characterize the relationship of authors to their ideas. Literary authors claimed authority for their writings, because the writings were products of intense, self-conscious labor (unlike the labor required by an utterance), because their writings supposedly expressed their own imaginary worlds, and because they considered themselves unique; and they claimed proprietorship over their texts (their "works") in part because original texts that the culture consumed had come to represent money. Behind this concept of the literary work as a property was the supposition that the self was an autonomous source of ideas.

The copyright was the positive side of the text's status as the property of its author; the negative side was the punishment that could be given the author for subverting the state or Church through unlawful writing. According to Foucault, "Speeches and books were assigned real authors, other than mythical or important religious figures, only when the author became subject to punishment and to the extent that his discourse was considered transgressive" (124). State censorship accompanied the recognition of the power of the printed text, and in opposition to censorship Milton argued in *Areopagitica* (1644) that the book represented "reason itself":

Books are not absolutely dead things, but doe contain a potencie of life in them to be as active as that soule was whose progeny they are; nay, they do preserve as in a violl the purest efficacie and extraction of that living intellect that bred them. I know they are as lively, and as vigorously productive, as those fabulous Dragons teeth; and being sown up and down, may chance to spring up armed men. And yet on the other hand unlesse warinesse be us'd, as good almost kill a Man as kill a good Book; who kills a Man kills a reasonable creature, Gods image; but hee who destroyes a good Booke, kills reason it selfe, kills the image of God, as it were, in the eye. (492)

An utterance in an oral culture could certainly have been considered transgressive—subversive or blasphemous—but its temporary existence did not threaten the state to the degree that the printed text did, with its permanence, reproducibility, and potentially unlimited audience. The very debate over censorship, over the possible danger of books to the authority of church and state, increased the authority of the author.

The technology that made possible the book made possible the extended narrative created by one person, a narrative that was not necessarily "true." Since the novel, developing in the newly print-literate sixteenth century with such picaresque works as the anonymous *Lazarillo de Tormes* and then, in 1605, with the much more complex first volume of *Don Quixote*, did not obtain its value from its approximation to the truth of actual occurrences, it needed an author to "authorize" its value, to take responsibility for it. And since the book was "less like an utterance and more like a thing," a thing that told a story with the storyteller absent, the author's name became intrinsic to its identity, serving as an indicator of the fiction's relationship with other texts. The novel developed as an imitation of history, and its author was the creator, the little god, who made the fictive world in the same way that the transcendent God made the material world of "reality."

The attention given the self from the time of the invention of the printing press supported the development of literary study as a discipline. But that attention did not derive solely from the availability of books. Literary study became a discipline in opposition to science, to technology, and to industry, all of which appeared to humanist scholars to neglect the self, that aspect of the human being which the culture connected with God.

The secularization of the culture involved the distancing of God from nature (Keller 54). The motivation behind the seventeenth-century argument that the universe was comprehensible in terms of physical "laws" which ultimately human beings could understand was the same as that of Lucretius, who stated in the first century B.C. that the world consisted of atoms: it was a desire to rid humanity of "irrational" fears of the supernatural. However, this philosophical transformation of nature into a mechanical universe of inert matter, which functioned to assure man of his power over nature, produced the human alienation from it that Pascal expressed in his *Pensées*:

Man is a mere reed, the weakest thing in nature; but he is a thinking reed. The entire universe need not arm itself to crush him; a vapour, a drop of water, is sufficient to cause his death. But if the universe were to crush him, man would still be nobler than his destroyer, because he knows that he dies, and also the advantage that the universe has over him; but the universe knows nothing of this.

Our whole dignity, therefore, consists in thought. From this we must rise, not from space and time which we cannot fill. Let us endeavour then to think aright, this is the principle of morality. (Pascal 488, trans. Warrington 110)

To believe that nature was only matter operating according to absolute laws was automatically to extract the human mind, as spirit, from it. And in defense against that universe, the culture ascribed human dignity to thought. Through the "death of nature," resulting in the seventeenth century from the disappearance of the medieval belief that the earth was a living organism, nature became matter to be manipulated by human beings and exploited for human purposes in the commercial capitalism sanctioned by Baconian science. Bacon's reorientation of science from individual work to a collaborative enterprise aimed at social improvement had served to legitimate the technological use of nature by those in possession of natural resources (Merchant 111). Bacon, throughout his philosophical works, argued that science's purpose was actively to explore nature for new knowledge that would contribute to the material improvement of the human condition. With the culture's increasing technology, that exploration turned into exploitation. In the industrial age, those who were in control of natural resources were in control of human resources—human bodies and their labor. Thus the mechanical universe, in which the human mind was presumed to be separate from the body, and the human spirit separate from matter, became the model for the industrialized socioeconomic world where, as Marx showed, human beings were alienated from their own work, which belonged to the marketplace and had monetary value. The spirit/matter dualism appeared everywhere.

The domination of nature in the seventeenth century was characterized by analysis, that is, by breaking down a problem into its component parts and isolating each part from its environment for investigation, and by specialization. In Bacon's utopian fiction *The New Atlantis*, which presented a society governed by scientists, the research institute called Salomon's House had as its purpose "the knowledge of Causes, and secret motions of things" (3: 156). To the accomplishment of this end it was divided into separate laboratories— caves, towers, lakes, wells, houses, baths, orchards, parks, brewhouses, and so forth—for the study of separate aspects of nature, such as metals, weather, fish, and disease. (3: 156–164). And there were specialists for each.

The removal of God from nature that occurred with the conception of the mechanical, material universe made for a contest between scientists who sought truth in fundamental physical laws and humanists who sought truth in expressions of the human spirit. To scientists, literature perhaps benefited society by refining human beings emotionally and spiritually, but it did not contribute to society's real knowledge. To humanists, science ignored human reality and God. At its extremes, the humanist's fear of science and the scientist's contempt for the humanities produced the split between the humanities and the sciences that has continued into the twentieth century, the split C. P. Snow defined in his 1959 lecture "The Two Cultures."

Representational aesthetics, issuing from the dualist separation of observer from world, reflected the opposition of spirit and matter in the artwork's expression of an idea that transcended the material world represented. The idea was the "content" within the text's form which rendered fiction valuable to the culture. As "feigned history" acquired importance to a culture that considered scientific and historical accounts of events to be concerned with the material, literature became an object of study. No less than poetry, which concealed its meaning in a "treasury of eloquence," the novel demanded interpretation: its value depended upon society's perception that it contained a message. It demanded interpretation because, unlike history, it issued from the imagination of its author, from its author's soul, and its words were worth pondering for access to that message. As a consequence of the notion that some secular works merited preservation—which accompanied the notion that those secular works merited interpretation—"literature" came to be a category (Fiedler, *What Was Literature?* 120).

The spirit/matter dualism, then, set up a multitude of oppositions relevant to texts: rhetorical/nonrhetorical; poetry/prose; literature/science; subjectivity/objectivity; fiction/history; meaning/events; content/form; idea/words; spiritual truth/material truth. And the concordant self/world dualism set up the oppositions of author/text and reader/text.

As Raymond Williams pointed out in *Marxism and Literature*, the word *litterature* had been used in English since the fourteenth century to mean "literacy," which itself did not enter the language as a word until the nineteenth century, after "literature" had become a category of texts. Even the word *literary*, in the language since the seventeenth century, was used to mean reading ability until the category of literature was developed. On its way to being a classificatory word denoting a product, *literature* meant "humane learning," the learning of the upper classes, which was generally directed toward writings in the classical languages. According to Williams, various interacting forces produced the Romantic shift in the meaning of *literature*, which for a while included all books, to "imaginative writing": the increasing nationalism, which yielded the concept of tradition; the development of the notion of taste and the associated concept of the aesthetic; and the require-

ments of creativity and originality attached to the category (45–54). The result of the interaction of these forces was the definition of "literature" as a
body of imaginative works that exhibited creativity and originality on the part
of their authors, that were read by an educated social class, and that derived
value from their differences from texts representing actual events in the material world.

The Industrial Revolution was partly responsible for this new definition of
literature. By turning the results of human labor into products, or commodities, the Industrial Revolution not only encouraged consideration of
various kinds of writings as various kinds of commodities but also clarified
the difference between history, which served as a practical account of events,
and literature, or imaginative writing, which could serve as an escape from
that unattractive, material world. The Industrial Revolution yielded as one of
its byproducts the reorientation away from the world and toward the self that
characterized the writing of the Pre-Romantics, who exalted the individual in
rebellion against the industrial culture. Their glorification of the uniqueness of
each individual and their appreciation for the individual's expression of emotions resulted in the new aesthetic requirement of "originality" and the new
concept of the literary genius as a little god, creator of the poetic universe
whose mysteries were not fully comprehensible. In the words of Edward
Young (from *Conjectures on Original Composition*, published in 1759):
"There is something in poetry beyond prose-reason; there are mysteries in it
not to be explained, but admired; which render mere prose-men infidels to
their divinity. And here pardon a second paradox; viz. 'Genius often then
deserves most to be praised, when it is sure to be condemned; that is, when its
excellence, from mounting high, to weak eyes is quite out of sight' " (342).

In 1774, Alexander Gerard, a professor in King's College, Aberdeen, published *An Essay on Genius*, in which he defined "genius" as "the faculty of
invention" (Gerard 8) and distinguished between the ends toward which that
invention was directed: the discovery of truth, belonging to the sciences, and
the production of beauty, belonging to the arts. In so doing he expressed a
shift in connotation which the verb *to invent* underwent during this period
from its Latin meaning of "to find" to its modern meaning of "to create." For
Gerard, who was articulating ideas in the air among the poets, the two kinds
of genius operated differently from each other, the artistic genius working
through taste, and the scientific genius through the understanding (318–19).
By emphasizing "invention" as the necessary characteristic of genius, Gerard
implied that the individual was an originator of ideas and that the mind operated independently of physical laws. By separating beauty from truth as ends
to which the two kinds of genius aspired, Gerard reinforced the culture's
assumption that science led to real knowledge—that is, information regarding

material laws—whereas the arts led to beauty, whose appreciation would inevitably be secondary to the satisfaction of material needs. Gerard's distinction between taste and understanding picked up Bacon's distinction between imagination and reason and anticipated a major argument of Immanuel Kant.

Kant's three critiques—*The Critique of Pure Reason, The Critique of Practical Reason,* and *The Critique of Judgement*—divided the human mind into three parts: the understanding, the conscience, and the aesthetic judgment, or taste. Expressing a dichotomy between writing that issued from and appealed to the imagination and writing that served practical purposes, Kant in his *Critique of Judgement* (1790) defined the aesthetic judgment as a judgment of purely subjective "taste," a "contemplative" judgment which considered "beautiful" only those works serving no useful function (55). For Kant, "[the satisfaction] of taste in the Beautiful is alone a disinterested and *free* satisfaction; for no interest, either of sense or of reason, here forces our assent" (54). An aesthetic object must be judged only according to itself, not according to any external standard (84).

Kant's "aesthetic judgement" elevated for appreciation primarily texts that apparently had no political or social purpose and neglected consideration of political and social forces upon them. The effect of his argument was to remove literature from history: by associating beauty with works that inspired contemplation rather than action, Kant made literature transcendent to events in time. According to Kant, "A judgement of taste, then, in respect of an object with a definite internal purpose, can only be pure, if either the person judging has no concept of this purpose, or else abstracts from it in his judgement" (83). These arguments supported the development of literary study as a discipline apparently concerned with the timeless and the universal in ontologically autonomous literary works.

With the spread of print literacy, with the increased self-consciousness it brought to the culture, with the concept of the poem as printed text, the function of poetry became, for some writers, less that of influencing the audience and more that of expressing the poet's private emotions. William Wordsworth, John Stuart Mill, and Samuel Taylor Coleridge, like Kant, believed that poetry ceased to be poetry when it was perceived to have a practical purpose. In 1800 Wordsworth defined poetry as "the spontaneous overflow of powerful feelings" (266), and in 1833 Mill separated "poetry" from "eloquence" in terms of poetry's orientation toward the self rather than toward an audience. For Mill, eloquence was "heard," poetry "overheard"; poetry was "feeling confessing itself to itself, in moments of solitude" (109). Coleridge discriminated poetry from all other written composition because the poem provided delight as a unity unto itself, "the parts of which mutually support and explain each other; all in their proportion harmonizing with, and supporting the purpose and known influences of metrical arrangement" (13). The difference between the poem and other texts, for Coleridge, lay in the wholeness of the poem: "A poem is that species of composition, which is opposed to works of science, by proposing for its *immediate* object pleasure, not truth; and from all other species (having *this* object in common with it) it is discriminated by proposing to itself such delight from the *whole*, as is compatible with a distinct gratification from each component *part*" (13). And if the poem was a whole, containing meaning in the arrangement of its "parts," its meaning was above history.

The Critique of Judgement and other Romantic writings on poetic composition had the effect of establishing art as an activity fulfilling a fundamental human need—that of interpreting reality, obtaining the meaning of events. Although the Romantic poets, as well as post-Romantic writers of various genres, addressed a secular world, their assumption that things of the world signified something beyond matter, which they as poets could reveal, raised their status, at least in their own eyes, to that once held by priests. For Wordsworth, the poet could "see into the life of things" (114). Bacon, Gerard, Kant, Wordsworth, Mill, and Coleridge, in diverse ways, associated with spirit the soul, divinity, subjectivity, fictive writing, poesy, interest in antiquity, the arts, taste (that is, the category of the aesthetic), the imagination, the useless, beauty, and transcendent truth. And they associated with matter the body, the material world, objectivity, factual writing, science, history, reason, the useful, and empirical truth.

In the defining of literature in the course of the next hundred years—that is, in the narrowing of the category to include only imaginative texts—certain influential thinkers from A. C. Bradley, at the end of the century, through the American New Critics gave those works the status of autonomous objects, whose interpretation could exclude consideration of the circumstances of their creation, of their intended audience, or of their political assumptions and assertions. The separation of the aesthetic from reason, by the privileging of the aesthetic over the rational analysis of phenomena, justified the activity of interpreting the interpretation (the artwork) to obtain knowledge of the transcendent.

2

Dualism and
"Culture"

But education is a higher word [than instruction]; it implies an action upon our mental nature, and the formation of a character; it is something individual and permanent, and is commonly spoken of in connexion with religion and virtue. When, then, we speak of the communication of Knowledge as being Education, we thereby really imply that Knowledge is a state or condition of mind; and since cultivation of mind is surely worth seeking for its own sake, we are thus brought once more to the conclusion, which the word "Liberal" and the word "Philosophy" have already suggested, that there is a Knowledge, which is desirable, though nothing come of it, as being of itself a treasure, and a sufficient remuneration of years of labour.

—Cardinal Newman, *The Idea of a University*

Culture is then properly described not as having its origin in curiosity, but as having its origin in the love of perfection; it is *a study of perfection*. It moves by the force, not merely or primarily of the scientific passion for pure knowledge, but also of the moral and social passion for doing good. . . .

. . . Religion says: *The kingdom of God is within you*; and culture, in like manner, places human perfection in an *internal* condition, in the growth and predominance of our humanity proper, as distinguished from our animality.

—Matthew Arnold, *Culture and Anarchy*

Merdre!

—Alfred Jarry, *Ubu Roi*

In 1852 John Henry Newman delivered the Dublin address titled "Knowledge Its Own End"; it became part of his influential *The Idea of a University* (1873), in which he argued that the object of education was knowledge itself and that "liberal knowledge" refused "to be *informed* . . . by any end, or absorbed into any art, in order duly to present itself to our contemplation"

26

(Newman 81). Quoting Aristotle, Newman distinguished between liberal knowledge, which gave nothing of consequence beyond the knowing, and useful knowledge, which yielded revenue. Because he associated education with development of character and ultimately with knowledge of God, his idea of a university supported the cause of liberal arts—and more specifically that of the humanities—when science invaded the traditional college curriculum in the latter half of the nineteenth century; his idea thereby underpinned the emerging discipline of literary study.

For Newman, all branches of liberal knowedge were unified into a whole, because the subject matter was the work of God (75), and the purpose of the university was to acquaint students with that body of knowledge, which was more or less fixed: the university should dedicate itself to teaching, "to the diffusion and extension of knowledge rather than its advancement" (xxxvii). The familiarity with "the great outlines of knowledge" formed in students a philosophical habit of mind characterized by "freedom, equitableness, calmness, moderation, and wisdom" (76). A liberal education, appropriate to a gentleman, a free man, differed from a commercial or professional education in the same way that "liberal" differed from "servile": "servile work" meant "bodily labour, mechanical employment, and the like, in which the mind has little or no part" (Newman 80). The liberal, or philosophical, education aimed at the comprehension of general ideas, whereas the mechanical devoted itself to the particular and to the external. Wrote Newman, "I only say that Knowledge, in proportion as it tends more and more to be particular, ceases to be Knowledge. . . . Not to know the relative disposition of things is the state of slaves or children; to have mapped out the Universe is the boast, or at least the ambition, of Philosophy." Liberal knowledge was "an acquired illumination . . . a habit, a personal possession, and an inward endowment" (85). In order to develop the "eye of the mind," as opposed to "the bodily eye" (116), which nature made for apprehending material objects, the university had to impose discipline, whose end was to "expel the excitements of sense by the introduction of those of the intellect." Thus without promising a heavenly reward, the university served to rescue "the victims of passion and self-will" (141).

Newman's privileging of the intellectual over the physical or mechanical expressed the fundamental spirit/matter dualism that for humanists had long relegated science to the pursuit of a lesser truth. To Newman literature differed from natural science in that literature expressed subjective truth, whereas science expressed objective truth; literature had to do with "thoughts," whereas science had to to with "things"; literature used language "in its full compass, as including phraseology, idiom, style, composition, rhythm, eloquence," whereas science used words merely as "symbols"

(206–7). Knowledge could be divided into the natural and the supernatural, for which reason the two kinds of knowledge could never contradict each other: the physicist, concerned with matter, would not seek to learn the origin of the universe; the theologian, concerned not with nature itself, would supply the reasons for natural phenomena, since the theologian contemplated "the world, not of matter, but of mind; the Supreme Intelligence; souls and their destiny; conscience and duty; the past, present, and future dealings of the Creator with the creature" (326). The opposition of philosophy or literature to science paralleled the opposition of theology to science: the focus on ideas opposed the focus on material particulars, just as the subjective opposed the objective, liberal education opposed commercial or professional education, and intellectual interests opposed the passions. Since the subject matter of knowledge was the work of the Creator, the end of a liberal arts education was knowledge of God.

Matthew Arnold translated Newman's "education" into "culture," or "the best that is known and thought in the world" (*Complete Works* 3: 270), which gave "sweetness and light." "He who works for sweetness and light, works to make reason and the will of God prevail" (5: 112). Culture enabled human beings, "by means of its spiritual standard of perfection," to escape the state of Philistinism, which manifested itself in wealth and in the desire for wealth: to cultured human beings, wealth was but machinery (5: 97). Culture was to Philistinism as humanity was to animality. And culture, by bringing us to "right reason," constituted the principle of authority against anarchy (5: 126). Thus Arnold saw culture as the expression of spiritual values, whose authority was God.

It was the critic who took responsibility for bringing culture to bear on the "human situation"—but not on politics. Criticism for Arnold meant the "disinterested endeavour to learn and propagate the best that is known and thought in the world" (3: 283), and criticism proved its disinterestedness by leaving alone "all questions of practical consequences and applications" (3: 270). Good critics operated in a realm above politics, in the sphere of the ideal, where they could do their "best spiritual work": "to keep man from a self-satisfaction which is retarding and vulgarising, to lead him towards perfection, by making his mind dwell upon what is excellent in itself, and the absolute beauty and fitness of things" (3: 271). Yet, Arnold argued, most people, because they lived practically, did not recognize their need for critics, without whom truth and the highest culture were unavailable.

Arnold's definition of culture overlapped his definition of poetry (that is, literature), the function of which was to replace religion and philosophy in interpreting life (9: 161–62). The study of poetry provided "the benefit of clearly feeling and of deeply enjoying the really excellent," to which, "as the *Imitation* [*The Imitation of Christ*] says, whatever we may read or come to know, we always return" (9: 156). Such excellence could not be recreated by the literary critic, as it inhered in the words themselves. For that reason—in Arnold's elaboration on Aristotle—poetry was superior to history for "possessing a higher truth and a higher seriousness," the superior character of which "in the matter and substance of the best poetry [was] inseparable from the superiority of diction and movement marking its style and matter" (9: 171).

In 1883–84, after Darwin's publication of *The Descent of Man* (1871), and in response to Thomas Huxley's advocacy of science in higher education, Arnold gave a lecture titled "Literature and Science" at various American universities; in it he declared that only "humane letters" could relate the results of science to human endeavor. Answering Huxley's charge that medieval education had neglected knowledge of nature, Arnold defended the Church, saying that the knowledge delivered by Scripture had "so deeply engaged men's hearts, by so simply, easily, and powerfully relating itself to their desire for conduct, their desire for beauty" (10: 66). Now, with science gaining respectability, the study of the humanities, which had the power to engage the emotions, was as necessary as ever. Quoting Darwin, Arnold argued that when men had "duly taken in the proposition that their ancestor was a 'hairy quadruped furnished with a tail and pointed ears, probably arboreal in his habits,'" human beings would still desire a means to relate that proposition to "the sense in us for conduct, and to the sense in us for beauty" (10: 64–65). Because science was incapable of doing this, it would finally weary the rest of society with its facts.

Cartesian dualism dichotomized everything. For most of the major thinkers of the period between the seventeenth and twentieth centuries, all phenomena could be characterized as partaking either of the spiritual aspect of reality or of the material and could thereby be ranked in terms of "higher" or "lower," superior or inferior. Those "things" that belonged to the material usually displayed a "mechanical" nature, just as the Newtonian universe did to the observer, and yielded "facts."

Newman and Arnold alike supported the humanities with theological fervor, for to them the humanities offered knowledge of God; the sciences did not. That fundamental distinction in the objects of study, spirit for literature and matter for science, categorized all that they considered. In Newman's essays liberal knowledge opposed practical knowledge: a liberal education provided character development, an "illumination," whereas a commercial or professional education provided training for servile work, such as bodily labor and mechanical employment. Literature expressed thoughts, science disclosed things; literature was subjective, science objective. Philosophy developed the eye of the mind, nature the eye of the body. In Arnold's essays culture opposed Philistinism, poetry opposed history, humane letters opposed science, human emotions opposed inert facts, humanity opposed animality. And culture brought "sweetness and light," whereas the lack thereof presumably left society in darkness.

The Cartesian supposition that the individual could be an objective observer of an external reality replicated itself in Arnold's assertion that the cultured critic, aware of the best that was known and thought in the world, could be a "disinterested" commentator on society—that is, could speak the truth by remaining above politics and not engaging in the action of practical life. Because they considered the world of such knowledge, which for Newman was an end in itself, separate from and superior to the world of commerce (and of self-interest, passion, and hunger), Arnold and Newman were, perhaps unintentionally, upholding the established political structure, despite Arnold's zeal for bettering the middle class. And, of course, not all students could afford the luxury of obtaining an education that supplied no material benefit; only "gentlemen," whose material wants were already satisfied, could enjoy the contemplation of "useless" ideas. Arnold's and Newman's belief that some kinds of discourse implied no ideology and their belief that the purpose of knowledge was contemplation provided for literary scholars in both England and America a theoretical justification for the independence of the university from politics. In effect, it isolated the discipline of literary study from many of the culture's social concerns.

By linking the humanities with character development, or development of the soul, Newman and Arnold reinforced the soul/body dichotomy, to the neglect of the body's material needs. Newman's argument that liberal knowledge brought "illumination" and Arnold's that the knowledge of the best known and thought in the world brought "sweetness and light" metaphorically associated "culture" with knowledge of God. In fact, their identification of culture with a "spiritual standard of perfection" merged the objective of humanistic study with the objective of Christianity: to purify the soul in a fallen world.

Newman and Arnold were not the only Victorian thinkers to offer a rationale for humanistic learning, nor did they think alike with respect to religion, but by virtue of their positions in society they became well-known spokesmen for the liberal arts. Newman, a tutor at Oriel College at Oxford in the 1820s and a minister of the Church of England, was a convert to Catholicism (in 1845) devoted to spreading traditional Christianity in the form of a revealed religion with an unchangeable set of beliefs. In 1849, he gathered together a group of highly educated priests to found the first English house of the Congregation of the Oratory, in imitation of St. Philip Neri's establishment of Oxford. Then in 1851, after giving advice on how to set up a university for Irish Catholics, Newman accepted the position of Rector of the new Catholic University at Dublin, and the following year he delivered the first five lectures collected in *The Idea of a University*. Pope Leo XIII made him a cardinal of the Roman church in 1879 (Newman vii-xv).

Arnold, influenced by Newman since their meeting in 1844, accepted many of his ideas about culture, criticism, and liberalism, though he differed from him regarding the value of dogma.[1] Educated at Oxford, Arnold was appointed by the British government in 1851 to an inspectorship in the Education Department, in which position he remained the rest of his life. In 1857, after obtaining fame as a poet, he was elected to the Oxford Chair of Poetry, and at that time he began writing essays critical of the middle class and of the churches. In 1873, he published *Literature and Dogma* (*an essay towards a better apprehension of the Bible*), where he presented a means of escaping the dilemma of religious dogma or science: the consideration of Biblical language as "literary." "Culture" enabled the reader of the Bible to obtain "the right interpretation": "if conduct is, as it is, inextricably bound up with the Bible and the right interpretation of it, then the importance of culture becomes unspeakable. For if conduct is necessary (and there is nothing so necessary), culture is necessary" (*Complete Works*, 6: 162).

Both Newman and Arnold appealed initially to those in society who believed that liberal education served some of the same causes that religion served; yet their ideas on the value of liberal education were cited long into the twentieth century in England and America in very secular contexts. Their essays were printed and reprinted as cogent justifications for maintaining a philosophical distance between the university and the rest of society and for retaining the humanities as the center of the college curriculum. Newman's definition of a university was instrumental in the development of the concept of academic freedom: a university was a place "in which the intellect may safely range and speculate, sure to find its equal in some antagonistic activity, and its judge in the tribunal of truth. It is a place where inquiry is pushed forward, and discoveries verified and perfected, and rashness rendered innocuous, and error exposed, by the collision of mind with mind, and knowledge with knowledge" (quoted in Fellman 11).

In the United States, Newman's *Idea of a University* influenced even Daniel Coit Gilman, who, after actively supporting the Morrill land-grant proposal as a utilitarian in 1858, presided over the birth of the first research-oriented graduate school in the United States: the Johns Hopkins University. Despite his early utilitarian leanings, Gilman continued to believe that the

university should "be a place for the development of character" (quoted in
Veysey 161), a place for "the defense of ideality, the maintenance of spirituality" (Gilman 95), a place where "the spirit of repose" is cultivated:

> A society of the choicest minds produced in any country, engaged in receiving and
> imparting knowledge, devoted to the study of nature, the noblest monuments of
> literature, the marvelous abstractions of mathematical reasoning, the results of his-
> torical evidence, the progress of human civilization, and the foundations of re-
> ligious faith, will be at once an example of productive quietude and an incitement
> to the philosophic view of life, so important to our countrymen in this day. (Gil-
> man 100)

In his 1918 book *The Higher Learning in America*, Thorstein Veblen defined a university as "a seminary of the higher learning" (16), whose aim was
"to equip the student for the work of inquiry, not to give him facility in that
conduct of affairs that turns such knowledge to 'practical account'" (17).
Although Veblen differed from Newman in exalting scholarly and scientific
research over instruction, he inherited Newman's and Arnold's opposition of
the "higher" intellectual life to the "lower" practical (or business) life; he
argued for the removal of professional schools from the university, criticized
the "captains of erudition" (university presidents) for administering the university as if it were a corporation which trafficked "in merchantable instruction" (89), and attacked the society that entrusted the management of the
academy to men of wealth. For Veblen, "the pursuit of learning [was] a
species of leisure" in that it had no economic or pecuniary end (116).

Arnold's "The Study of Poetry" (1880) formed much of the basis of the
American New Criticism of the 1940s. In that essay he asked that critics seek
the "real estimate" of a poem, rather than the fallacious "historic estimate"
or the fallacious "personal estimate" (*Complete Works* 9: 163), anticipating
the attitudes of W. K. Wimsatt and Monroe C. Beardsley toward "the intentional fallacy" and "the affective fallacy" (Wimsatt 3–31). By this "real
estimate" critics could determine whether the work belonged to the "class of
the very best," the canon of world literature. Excellent poems of that class
could not be paraphrased, but instead had to be appreciated "in the verse of
the master" (Arnold, *Complete Works* 9: 170), because paraphrase, as
Cleanth Brooks was to write over sixty years later, was "heresy" (*Well-
Wrought Urn* 201). Arnold's view that poetry would replace religion in the
interpretation of life, which for Arnold meant that poetry was "the strongest
part of our religion," became, in Wallace Stevens's atheism: "After one has
abandoned a belief in god, poetry is that essence which takes its place as life's
redemption" (158).

The language of Newman and Arnold disclosed connections among Cartesian dualism, religion, and "culture," limited in Arnold's use of the term to the arts and humanities. The Cartesian separation of the observer from the object of observation supported Newman's and Arnold's mutual belief that the intellectual life could distance itself from the practical life and that therefore the university could and should distance itself from society. Truth, in the Cartesian paradigm, was obtainable through "objectivity," which was achieved only by such separation. The Cartesian—and Christian—supposition that the spiritual was superior to the material supported Arnold's confidence in the ability of the disinterested critic, steeped in the best known and thought in the world, to know and communicate truth. And truth was absolute.

In the dualist paradigm, when art and literature represented reality mimetically, when reality was considered external, Arnold could argue convincingly that literature interpreted life, perhaps more satisfactorily than did religion as religion waned among the intellectuals, and that the study of poetry related events to the human sense of conduct and desire for beauty. Yet at the very time that Arnold was working out his argument that "culture" brought moral benefit, painters, shortly to be followed by avant-garde writers, were abandoning the realist aesthetic and were turning away from the best known and thought—or painted—in the world; they were attempting to rid art of its association with moral values. Artists and writers, from Flaubert and Mallarmé in France through Whistler and Wilde in England, advocated "art for art's sake"; and in 1901 A. C. Bradley, professor of poetry at Oxford, delivered the address "Poetry for Poetry's Sake," which disconnected literature from politics (as Kant had attempted to do a hundred years before) and from morality. But Bradley differed from the artists and writers in his motivation: the avant-garde (some from the left and others from the right) initiated through their work an attack on bourgeois values, whereas Bradley, by divorcing aesthetics from politics, turned the depoliticized art and literature into objects of study in an academic system that by its own idealized separateness from politics reinforced the political status quo.

The interpretation of reality had become increasingly problematical during the nineteenth century, as reality ceased to appear objectively definable, preorganized, rationally comprehensible, capable of depiction on a flat surface from a fixed point of view. Since the Renaissance, painters had employed linear perspective to present an external reality which they could capture "accurately" on canvas, an external reality which the print culture characterized mainly by its visible features. They accomplished such naturalism by quantifying space, that is, by conceiving of the visual field as a plane in which all the components of the field were mathematically related to each other according to the position of the painter. Reality was comprehensible to them. Painting between the seventeenth century and the early nineteenth reflected the dualist paradigm wherein the subject controlled the object: it was the world of imperialism, capitalism, and exploitation of natural resources, in which individuals conquered foreign territory, amassed wealth, and used the products of the earth for industry; it was the world of Baconian science, in which man tortured nature's secrets from her (Bacon 4: 298). In this age of rationalism, scientists and humanists alike considered the self distinct from and of greater importance than the surrounding material reality, and painters expressed that dualism both in the content of their paintings and in the realist form, achieved by the painters' distance from—and independence of—the visual field.

But after the middle of the nineteenth century, after the *Origin of Species*, that paradigm was beginning to lose hold. The Impressionists, in rebellion against the official art of Paris, exhibited their own work together in 1874, in a Salon des Refusés, and thereby initiated a revolution in the art world which took painting from realism to abstraction by 1915. Leaving their studios to paint outdoors, where they began studying the effects of light empirically, they came to recognize their subjective involvement in the visual field: that is, the impossibility of separating the observer from the object of observation. The Post-Impressionists explored the implications of the Impressionists' discoveries and, in anticipation of the discoveries of early twentieth-century scientists, abandoned the Newtonian concept of an objectively definable external reality, which traditional painters had represented through linear perspective.

Whistler, Degas, Monet, and Matisse shifted the artist's viewpoint to dislocate human activity from the center of the canvas to the edge and to picture events from unconventional angles. Whistler, Monet, and Cézanne merged objects with environment. Van Gogh, Gauguin, and Bonnard called attention to color as the medium of aesthetic representation, and Delaunay and Kandinsky gave color autonomy in twentieth-century abstraction. Monet, Signac, and Seurat showed greater interest in the function and composition of light than in the object they were ostensibly depicting. Manet, Cézanne, and Matisse abandoned linear perspective to emphasize the flatness of the canvas (see Clay). Their reorientation of focus from the external reality to the process of perceiving or depicting phenomena moved the art world toward expression of the new paradigm, that of a relativistic holism, in which scientists, philosophers, and writers would look to the culture's process of constructing reality. Decades later, James Joyce, Virginia Woolf, and William Faulkner demonstrated the inextricability of self from world in their stream-of-consciousness writing, which merged self and world in a character's mind.

In the early twentieth century Picasso liberated painting from representation completely in a series of steps from the expressionist paintings of his Blue

Period, through the cubism of *Les Demoiselles d'Avignon* and the *Portrait of Daniel-Henry Kahnweiler*, to the collages of 1912. The collages, which represented nothing other than themselves and deliberately confused art and the practical world, questioned the concept of art itself. What did art do, what was its function in society, if it did not re-present illusionistically an external reality? How could it be evaluated? What made it precious? In 1912 the Italian painter Giorgio de Chirico wrote:

> What will the aim of future painting be? The same as that of poetry, music, and philosophy: to create previously unknown sensations; to strip art of everything routine and accepted, and of all subject matter, in favor of an aesthetic synthesis; completely to suppress man as a guide, or as a means to express symbol, sensation, or thought, once and for all to free itself from the anthropomorphism that always shackles sculpture; to see everything, even man, in its quality of *thing*. (Chipp 397)

Meanwhile, in the world of avant-garde literature, Alfred Jarry and the later Futurists and Dadaists were participating in the shift in paradigm in another way. In their revolt against bourgeois morality and establishment art, they rejected the assumption that art supplied spiritual refreshment to those capable of appreciating it, and in so doing they rejected the spirit/matter dualism that had given definition to literature and fine art since the Scientific Revolution. In 1896 Jarry presented in Paris his play *Ubu Roi*, which opened with the shouted word "Merdre!"—or "Shit!" (*merde*) slightly misspelled. In 1897 Mallarmé wrote "Un Coup de dés" ("A Throw of the Dice"), in which he broke up the traditional linear order of words on the printed page to picture his theme chirographically; in its preface he called the reader's attention to the poem as a printed object whose white space mattered as much as the words. In 1909 Filippo Tommaso Marinetti inaugurated Italian Futurism with a massive publicity campaign through newspapers, posters, and manifestos, of which the first was "The Foundation and Manifesto of Futurism," appearing in its entirety on the front page of Europe's major newspaper *Le Figaro*; in it he declared: "We will glorify war . . . destroy museums, libraries, and fight against moralism, feminism, and all utilitarian cowardice" (Chipp 286). In 1911 the American Gertrude Stein published *Tender Buttons*, which contained such paragraphs as the following: "A kind in glass and a cousin, a spectacle and nothing strange a single hurt color and an arrangement in a system to pointing. All this and not ordinary, not unordered in not resembling. The difference is spreading" (161).

In Zurich, in 1916, the Dadaists demanded "the elimination of concepts of property in the new art" (Chipp 382) and the dismissal of bourgeois aesthetic values:

DADA
stands on
the side of the revolutionary
Proletariat
Open up at last
your head
Leave it free
for the
demands of our age
Down with art
Down with
bourgeois intellectualism
Art is dead
Long live
the machine art
of Tatlin
DADA
is the
voluntary destruction
of the
bourgeois world of idea

(Chipp 376)

In 1924 the Frenchman André Breton, turning away from the machine world
to explore the unconscious, advocated the writing of "Surrealist" poetry,
"dictated by thought, in the absence of any control exercised by reason, ex-
empt from any aesthetic or moral concern" (26).

In abandoning representation as the purpose of art, the revolutionary
painters and writers challenged the culture's criteria for aesthetic judgment. In
obliterating the distinction between art and non-art, between art object and
event, they challenged the culture's notion of the preciousness of the artwork.
In frustrating the spectator's or the reader's desire for coherence and beauty,
they insulted the society that had originally defended art as an enterprise of
spiritual value to human beings. More fundamentally, however, these ico-
noclasts, who redefined (or undefined) art for the twentieth century, were
questioning the humanist-rationalist basis of Western culture since the Renaissance: the privileging of the rational over the irrational, of mind over body, of
spirit over matter.

What Arnold had put forth as the purpose of culture the avant-garde rejected. Arnold's appeal to "sweetness and light" and to "the best that is
known and thought in the world" held no authority for either the Futurists,
who advocated the destruction of museums and libraries as "cemeteries," or

the later Surrealists, who sought knowledge in automatic writing. Both Arnold and Newman had disparaged the concern with the material as "mechanical"; the Futurists glorified the machine. Arnold found poetry to be characterized by a "superiority of diction and movement marking its style and manner"; the Surrealists rejected "the reign of logic" (Chipp 413). For Arnold, poetry appealed to the human sense of conduct and the sense of beauty; for avant-garde painters and poets, art relinguished any connection it once had with morality and traditional beauty. For Arnold, the purpose of culture was to provide a "spiritual standard of perfection" for human beings; for de Chirico art must free itself from anthropomorphism, "to see everything, even man, in its quality of *thing*." For Arnold, the best poetry possessed "truth and seriousness" (*Complete Works* 9: 171); on stage, Pere Ubu shouted "Merdre!"

The Kantian-Arnoldian dissociation of the aesthetic from the political in literary discourse led "critics" to attempt to examine literary works independently of their political messages, and that tendency continued into the twentieth century, even, to some extent, in the consideration of avant-garde works. Yet the art of many of the aesthetic revolutionaries was explicitly political (as had been much nineteenth-century fiction). Arnold's definition of literature was founded upon the spirit/matter dichotomy of Cartesian dualism, and the avant-garde literature of the late nineteenth and early twentieth centuries presented an aggressive critique of that paradigm, a critique that often took the form of a political attack on capitalism. The assumptions that the poem gave a spiritual interpretation of a material reality, that the poem was an original creation by the poet, that language was a neutral medium of expression which the poet used to externalize preconceived ideas, that art was distinguishable from politics—all these dualist notions the early twentieth-century avant-garde rejected, in one way or another.

Separating the aesthetic from reason and morality, poets and painters declared art's superiority over rational analysis of phenomena in the obtaining and imparting of a knowledge that later both surrealists and psychoanalysts would associate with the unconscious. For many critics, the concept of the unconscious eventually subsumed that of the spirit as a source of the valuable "content" of the artwork, in justification of their continued activity of interpretation. The argument made by Arnold and then by Brooks that poetry could not be paraphrased functioned both to emphasize the mysterious nature of aesthetic knowledge and, paradoxically, to necessitate interpretation of the aesthetic object: the proclaimed mystery of art invited a culture once given to biblical exegesis to seek the artwork's hidden meanings.

The major shift in the perception, or construction, of reality, which was later to be described as the shift from the dualist paradigm to the holistic, had begun to call attention to itself with the publication of *On the Origin of Species* (1859) and *The Descent of Man* (1871), which destroyed the current scientific belief in the fixity of species, presented time as a force of fundamental and unpredictable change, ignored God in favor of natural selection as the agent of evolution, and made human consciousness an accident of natural history. After 1859, among intellectuals, the rationalist confidence in the God-given distinction between humans and animals started to erode, as did the belief in the distinction between soul and body and the belief in a Creator-God. Reality appeared to be a world of flux, where human beings had no guarantees of their control even over themselves. This was the reality that the Impressionists and Post-Impressionists had painted.

In 1882 Friedrich Nietzsche announced the "death" of God.

Have you not heard of that madman who lit a lantern in the bright morning hours, ran to the market place, and cried incessantly: "I seek God! I seek God!" —As many of those who did not believe in God were standing around just then, he provoked much laughter. Has he got lost? asked one. Did he lose his way like a child? asked another. Or is he hiding? Is he afraid of us? Has he gone on a voyage? emigrated? —Thus they yelled and laughed.

The madman jumped into their midst and pierced them with his eyes. "Whither is God?" he cried; "I will tell you. *We have killed him*—you and I. All of us are his murderers. But how did we do this? How could we drink up the sea? Who gave us the sponge to wipe away the entire horizon? What were we doing when we unchained this earth from its sun? Whither is it moving now? Whither are we moving? Away from all suns? Are we not plunging continually? Backward, sideward, forward, in all directions? Is there still any up or down? Are we not straying as through an infinite nothing? Do we not feel the breath of empty space? Has it not become colder? Is not night continually closing in on us? Do we not need to light lanterns in the morning? Do we hear nothing as yet of the noise of the grave-diggers who are burying God? Do we smell nothing as yet of the divine decomposition? Gods, too, decompose. God is dead. God remains dead. And we have killed him.

"How shall we comfort ourselves, the murderers of all murderers? What was holiest and mightiest of all that the world has yet owned has bled to death under our knives: who will wipe this blood off us? What water is there for us to clean ourselves? What festivals of atonement, what sacred games shall we have to invent? Is not the greatness of this deed too great for us? Must we ourselves not become gods simply to appear worthy of it? There has never been a greater deed; and whoever is born after us—for the sake of this deed he will belong to a higher history than all history hitherto."

Here the madman fell silent and looked again at his listeners, and they, too, were silent and stared at him in astonishment. At last he threw his lantern on the ground, and it broke into pieces and went out. "I have come too early," he said then; "my time is not yet. This tremendous event is still on its way, still wandering; it has not yet reached the ears of men. Lightning and thunder require time; the light of the stars requires time; deeds, though done, still require time to be seen and heard. This deed is still more distant from them than the most distant stars— *and yet they have done it themselves."* (181–2)

Although Nietzsche may not have been referring to Darwinism, his parable of the madman presented metaphorically the implications of the end of religious belief. The belief in a spiritual reality to give meaning and definition to events and things of the world had sustained Western civilization for several thousand years, since long before Homer recorded the activities of the Greek gods and goddesses. If Darwin was right—that the human species had evolved through the process of natural selection, that no god had set the agenda, and that consciousness had material origins—there was no dualism of spirit and matter. Indeed, a super-natural reality was but a human illusion, a human creation. The Darwinian assertion that matter had created spirit was equivalent to killing God, drinking up the sea, wiping away the horizon, unchaining the earth from its sun. In the absence of belief in a spiritual reality, a God, nothing had intrinsic meaning, for there was no origin of significance in the universe to bestow value on things. Was there still any up or down? If there was no God, there was no foundation for a vertical hierarchy of values, such as that established by the spirit/matter dualism which gave spiritual activities superiority over material activities, which made the life of the mind "higher" than the life of the body. There were no absolutes. The culture had plunged into the world of relativity, the world of relative values. According to Nietzsche, having killed God by the force of our intellect, we ourselves must become gods—inventing good and evil here and now (as the Existentialists later said)—merely to appear worthy of the deed.

The culture's notion of the "spiritual" had itself evolved between the seventeenth century and the nineteenth. For Descartes, the soul connected the human being with God: soul was to body as spirit (God) was to matter. Man was half spirit, half body, suspended in the Great Chain of Being between God and inanimate matter. But with the secularization of the culture the notion of "soul" gave way to that of "self," and the term "human spirit" referred, in secular contexts, to the "essentially" human, to those ideals, hopes, and fears that distinguished the human from the beast. Darwin's disclosure of the continuum between human and beast generated a critique of the notion of "essence," which Nietzsche initiated and to which Jean-Paul Sartre and, a generation later, Jacques Derrida contributed in the twentieth century. In short, the belief in a spiritual reality (God) distinct from a material reality had supported the belief in a human "nature," or human "essence," as well as the belief in the intrinsic meaning of phenomena. The acknowledgment that such dualism had been a cultural construction, traceable back beyond Plato, put into question the concepts of "human nature" and "self," as well as the notion of intrinsic meaning and values. For Sartre, existence preceded essence: "there is no human nature since there is no God to conceive it" (15). For Derrida, the universe had become "decentered" (249).[2] In the absence of a God to endow human beings, things, and events with transcendental (intrinsic) meaning, meaning was relative, a function of the culture's symbolic discourse.

But, said the madman, "I have come too early." A shift in paradigm takes time; it does not manifest itself in all aspects of the culture simultaneously. In fact, the shift that made an early appearance in the publication of *On the Origin of Species* has yet to dominate all of Western society, even at the end of the twentieth century. Darwin moved the discipline of natural history into modern biology by convincing his colleagues, in the course of a few decades, of the fact of evolutionary change and by proposing that the mechanism for evolution was natural selection (see Gould, "Darwinism Defined" 64). The Impressionists intuited the crisis in the Cartesian opposition of self and world and painted the self into the world. Yet to those still structuring reality according to the dualist paradigm, Darwin, Nietzsche, and the avant-garde artists threatened to undermine all that the culture held sacred. To the advocates of literary study in the university, Darwinian science represented not a new paradigm (which they could not have recognized) but rather the materialism of the old, over which the pursuit of spiritual truth should obviously take precedence. The respect that natural science was gaining in the latter half of the nineteenth century was for them an index to the culture's need for literature to relate scientific facts to the human sense of conduct and desire for beauty.

In **"Poetry for Poetry's Sake,"** Bradley called for the consideration of the poem "as it actually exists": "the succession of experiences—sounds, images, thoughts, emotions—through which we pass when we are reading as poetically as we can" (4). That experience was an end in itself, of intrinsic value: "its *poetic* value is this intrinsic worth alone" (4). Poetry could also serve other ends, such as providing culture, religion, or instruction, or it could further a good cause, but consideration of those ends, whether by the poet or by the reader, tended to lower the work's poetic value by taking the poem "out of its own atmosphere": "For its nature is to be not a part, nor yet a copy, of the real world (as we commonly understand that phrase), but to be *a world by itself, independent, complete, autonomous*; and to possess it fully you must enter that world, conform to its laws, and ignore for the time the beliefs, aims, and particular conditions which belong to you in the other world of reality" (5). Bradley then asserted the identity of content and form: to assume that the poem's value lay in either, independently of the other, was "heresy" (17). For poetry "is a spirit. It comes we know not whence. It will not speak at our bidding, nor answer in our language. It is not our servant; it is our master" (27).

For Bradley, thirty years after the publication of *The Descent of Man*, God was not dead: the naturalist Darwin had presented a materialist view of the biological world, a view which was incomplete in that it excluded consideration of the human spirit. Poetry, however, did address the human spirit, and because of religion's decreasing authority in the late nineteenth century, poetry would occupy the important position once commanded by scripture; it would be revered for itself alone by readers who were not necessarily believers in God. Poetry—that is, literature—offered a bounty of imaginative experiences to the reader who could ignore "the beliefs, aims, and particular conditions which belong to . . . the other world of reality"; and it thereby offered an escape from practical concerns, including morality.

The secular discipline of literary study began in opposition to science's materialist description of nature and depended upon the Cartesian opposition of subjectivity and objectivity. It depended upon the culture's belief that phenomena in the external reality had intrinsic (transcendent) meaning that the human subjectivity, speaking through literature, could disclose. Darwin proposed that human subjectivity had natural, rather than God-given, origins; Nietzsche said, "God is dead," meaning by the death of God the end of the belief in intrinsic values; the avant-garde painters and writers of the latter half of the century questioned the foundations for morality, objective perception, and art itself. Yet Bradley, and later the American New Critics, continued to function in the dualist paradigm, assuming that literature gave an interpretation of reality that a nonaesthetic text could not give. As the literature of the late nineteenth and early twentieth centuries became increasingly complex formally, in response to the upheaval of the paradigm shift, these critics found it not only convenient but logical to consider the work autonomous, concerned with itself as an aesthetic expression of "the other world," which at that time they believed was in crisis. When events ceased to have culturally agreed-upon meanings, then literature seemed to make events meaning*ful* for the culture; and because literature provided symbolic order, the literary work could be studied as "a world by itself." Literary study thus supported the dualist paradigm long into the twentieth century because its very existence as a discipline focused on "literature" as a body of "aesthetic" texts, distinct from fact-telling history, born of the individual subjectivity with the power to interpret or to make "meaningful" worldly events.

Newman had argued that liberal knowledge was desirable because it had no ulterior purpose other than the cultivation of the mind; Arnold had argued that culture made reason and the will of God prevail. Bradley, who inherited some of their attitudes toward letters, relieved poetry of moral obligation by declaring its value to inhere in itself alone. Sharing Newman's and Arnold's reverence toward literature, Bradley turned the poem into a secular icon to be worshipped not for what it did but for what it was: the poem belonged to the realm of the spirit; in its purest form it served no material ends. Four hundred years of print literacy had culminated in the complete extrication of the ("poetic") utterance from context and intention. Paradoxically, the secularization that print literacy had helped to bring about led, through Kant, to the treatment of the poem as an icon by literary critics who imagined that they had rescued poetry from morality. Bradley delivered the lecture "Poetry for Poetry's Sake" five years after Jarry had opened *Ubu Roi* on the Paris stage with "Merdre!"

Thus Bradley and the aesthetic revolutionaries came to the advocacy of art for art's sake by alternate routes: the sacred and the profane. Bradley, whose thinking was structured by Cartesian dualism, arrived by way of Kant, Newman, and Arnold, interpreting Kant's separation of the category of the aesthetic from that of the conscience to support poetry's independence of all practical and moral purposes. Although he appropriated Newman's and Arnold's connection of education and culture with the spirit, Bradley believed that by disconnecting poetry from morality he was secularizing literary study. Yet his location of the poem's meaning within the poem itself required the belief in a God to authorize that meaning, to fix it, to make it absolute.

The disjunction between Bradley's reasons for divorcing poetry from morality and the avant-garde artists' reasons for divorcing art from morality illustrated the ideological differences between the late nineteenth-century appreciators of art and the artists themselves. The avant-garde artists, particularly those of the early years of the twentieth century, signaled in their politically motivated art an iconoclasm. Bradley and the advocates of "poetry for poetry's sake," who considered the poem worthy of attention as a world in itself, "to be judged entirely from within" (Bradley 5), signaled in their removal of the poem from its political context a conservatism. The late nineteenth-century and early twentieth-century advocates for literary study in the universities implicitly supported the political status quo by treating the poem for its "poetic value" alone and by eliminating from consideration its social message, occasionally the major reason for its creation. They were late dualists in an art world that struggled to depict a new relativistic holism.

3

Science, the Humanities, and Higher Education

What a piece of work is a man! How noble in reason! how infinite in faculty! in form, in moving, how express and admirable! in action how like an angel! in apprehension how like a god!

—William Shakespeare, *Hamlet*

Man may be excused for feeling some pride at having risen, though not through his own exertions, to the very summit of the organic scale; and the fact of his having thus risen, instead of having been aboriginally placed there, may give him hopes for a still higher destiny in the distant future. But we are not here concerned with hopes or fears, only with the truth as far as our reason allows us to discover it. I have given the evidence to the best of my ability; and we must acknowledge, as it seems to me, that man with all his noble qualities, with sympathy which feels for the most debased, with benevolence which extends not only to other men but to the humblest living creature, with his god-like intellect which has penetrated into the movement and constitution of the solar system—with all these exalted powers—Man still bears in his bodily frame the indelible stamp of his lowly origin.

—Charles Darwin, *Descent of Man*

Paradigms replace each other slowly and unevenly. The paradigm shift from medieval to modern science culminated in the late seventeenth century, when Newton's concept of a mechanical universe in which laws governed matter was adopted by scientists. The proof of the paradigm's establishment in the scientific community was the scientists' shared commitment to a set of rules and standards by which they sought and evaluated scientific truth (Kuhn 10–11). To this model of reality, which dominated science for three hundred years, Bacon had contributed scientific induction as a method of obtaining knowledge and Descartes had contributed a philosophical articulation of the dualism of *res cogitans* and *res extensa*, which followed from the Middle Ages' spirit/matter dichotomy.

Bacon's separation of poesy from empirical science made the curriculum battles waged in American universities in the nineteenth century seem inevitable. For the separation allowed the disciplines of literary study and science to develop independently of each other, to the point that by 1860 the disciplines manifested ideologies that issued from different paradigms. Bacon and his fellow scientists sought verifiable truth through induction. Because of the habits they developed of proposing hypotheses, testing hypotheses, correcting hypotheses, and seeking to know that which the culture did not already know, scientists learned that the truth of nature was not contained in a fixed body of knowledge, that such truth was not always obvious or even accessible. Empirical knowledge had to be modified continually.

Yet the humanists expressed a medieval attitude toward truth well into the nineteenth century: that truth was unchanging and absolute, and that it should be accepted on the authority of belief. As Cartesian dualism moved the humanities toward a defense of the spiritual realm of human reality, the humanists—particularly literary scholars—accepted the notion that there were two kinds of truth, spiritual and material, of which the spiritual was superior, an assumption which legitimated two methods for pursuing truth: the theological-become-literary and the empirical.

Darwin's *On the Origin of Species* initiated another shift in paradigm,[1] this time to that of the relativist model in which things and events obtained meaning and definition relative to their function in a changing system. Though the full implications of that paradigm shift for other disciplines besides the natural sciences were not fully recognized for over fifty years, the book inspired in America a conflict between the advocates of the traditional classical education and the advocates of science in the universities. The cultural debate, however, took place not as a dispute between Newtonians and Darwinians, or even between dualists and early relativists, but rather between those holding medieval assumptions of the nature of truth and those holding mechanistic empirical assumptions. In the 1860s and 1870s, defenders of the classical curriculum argued from the premise that truth was contained in a fixed body of knowledge; their opponents (many of whom continued to interpret nature from a Christian viewpoint) argued for the inclusion of science in the curriculum from the premise that truth was debatable and discoverable in the study of nature. In 1877 Chauncey Wright characterized the two positions as having two "motives": the subjective and the objective. According to Wright, the ancients appealed to natural beliefs—"natural universal human interests and emotions"—for the verification of their theories, whereas the moderns, seeking objectivity, followed "interests which depend on acquired knowledge, and not on natural desires and emotions," and appealed to experimental evidence. Objectivity would be achieved when science ceased "to have man, his personal and social nature, as its central and controlling objects" (49). The humanists feared such objectivity for its not centering on the human.

Charles Darwin was not the initiator of the concept of evolution, but because in his *Origin of Species* he found the causes of evolution in nature alone, he precipitated a furious debate between the believers in a Creator God and the new believers in natural selection. In the course of the debate, literary study, which continued to define itself in opposition to science, sanctified a body of secular "literary" texts to interpret for their depiction of the human spirit, and modern biology became a discipline oriented toward a material world of flux. The antagonism between literature and science in the establishment of the modern curriculum reflected the stasis/flux debate that dominated science itself in the first half of the nineteenth century, in the protracted acknowledgment of a universe vast in time and space that apparently functioned without divine intervention. Darwin resolved the question for science and exacerbated it for the discipline of literary study, in which at the end of the century the question produced a dispute between literary evolutionists and literary critics.

Darwin developed his theory in consonance with various contemporary ideas: the discoveries in the fields of geology and natural history that pushed back the age of the earth millions of years, *laissez-faire* economics, utilitarianism, democracy, artificial selection, and the theory of food supply that Malthus had elaborated in his *Essay on Population* (1798). During the Enlightenment scientists had begun to persuade intellectuals that reason and direct observation of nature were the sole reliable methods for obtaining real knowledge and that thinkers must verify propositions before accepting or propagating them as truth. Their influence on the critical habits of mind of the literate populace brought about an erosion of authority for both church and monarchies. Newly confident of their capacity for critical thought, which print literacy had fostered and the Protestant Reformation had encouraged, the growing mercantile middle class became skeptical of and finally rebellious against the vertical social hierarchy characterizing European nations: they desired a more democratic political order. Postrevolutionary America and France therefore incorporated John Locke's 1689 proposal of a social contract among human beings who shared natural rights equally and Jean Jacques Rousseau's advocacy of equality among human beings into the American Declaration of Independence of 1776 and the French Declaration of the Rights of Man and of the Citizen of 1789, respectively, to shift authority for society's well-being from the state—that is, the monarchy—to the individual. The new individual liberty achieved by the radical restructuring of social and economic relationships carried with it a belief in the possible benefits of change, in social progress.

The enthusiasm for change was matched by a fear of change that was ultimately religious. And the nineteenth-century battle between the conservative upholders of traditional beliefs and the liberal empirical investigators of both society and nature was a battle between those who knew the world only in terms of God-granted vertical hierarchies, social and natural, and those who glimpsed a new order of things, a more horizontal order not only in society but perhaps also in nature, which the Great Chain of Being no longer seemed to characterize. The discoveries of the earth's age and of the earth's multitude of heretofore unclassified species of living creatures appeared to lessen the importance of the individual in relation to the cosmos. Many humanists discounted the significance of these discoveries by categorizing them as propositions valuable only insofar as they satisfied curiosity about the material residence of the human spirit. At root, however, this was a battle between the two modes of obtaining knowledge: the spiritual versus the material, the contemplative versus the practical, the mystical versus the experimental.

The stasis/flux issue became in natural science a debate between believers in a permanently ordered mechanical universe and believers in evolution. The eighteenth century had accommodated the knowledge of a vast and intricate universe to Christianity by reference to cosmic design: the clockwork universe implied a clockmaker. Newton argued in 1713 that the orderliness of the heavens gave proof of an intelligent agent, a Creator God. A century later William Paley continued the design argument in his *Natural Theology, or Evidences of the Existence and Attributes of the Deity collected from the Appearances of Nature* (1802), which Darwin knew well, asserting that in the same way a watch showed design, so did the universe: the entire natural world, down to the arms and legs and eyes of human beings and animals, all of which were composed of elaborate structures made up of parts functioning together for their required purposes, offered evidence of an intelligent designer.

Geological studies of the eighteenth and nineteenth centuries challenged the widespread belief in a Creator-designer by revealing that the earth did not exist in a static condition, that in fact nature had a history of perhaps millions of years. Georges Buffon, in his *Natural History*, the forty-four volumes of which were published between 1749 and 1804, showed that the earth had taken at least seventy thousand years for its molten rock to cool, thus undermining Archbishop Ussher's theory of 1650 that Creation took place in 4004 B.C. Buffon also described fossils as remains of organisms that lived in the distant past. Creationists had generally been unable to explain the existence of fossils, but some eighteenth-century and early nineteenth-century geologists did find means to reconcile the new empirical knowledge of the earth to Christian belief. Geologists of "catastrophism" (as William Whewell characterized them in 1837) held that catastrophic events, such as repeated volcanic eruptions and the upheaval of rock into mountain ranges, took place in the distant past before the appearance of human life on the earth's surface and that relative calm had governed the geological structure of the earth since then. In opposition to them, James Hutton presented what became known as "uniformitarianism" in his *Theory of the Earth with Proofs and Illustrations* of 1795, in which he attempted to show that the earth's surface was always changing, that the erosion, the deposition of sediments, and the hardening of rock by heat represented a continuing process.

In the field of natural history a theological debate raged between those believing in God's successive creation of separate species and those believing in evolution. Jean Baptiste de Lamarck and Erasmus Darwin, Charles Darwin's grandfather, rejected the explanation that successive creations had provided for the variety of species in favor of a naturalistic explanation: that organisms, evolving from simple to more complex forms, did so by adapting themselves to their environment to survive. In their evolutionism, however, they did not question the belief in a Creator God, for as eighteenth-century Deists they saw evolution as part of a cosmic mechanism begun at the time of the universe's creation. Lamarck went on to outline in 1809 a detailed theory of evolution according to the inheritance of acquired characteristics. The geologist Charles Lyell attacked Lamarck's theory of transmission in his *Principles of Geology* (1830–33) but indirectly lent support to the notion of evolution by arguing that natural forces had brought about the immense variation on the earth's surface over an immense period of time—the millions of years it would have taken for mankind to evolve from lowly forms of life. Science could not proceed with its empirical study of nature, said Lyell, if it attributed events to divine interference or miracles (R. Young 3). Lyell was in turn attacked in 1844 in the anonymous *Vestiges of the Natural History of Creation*, later attributed to Robert Chambers, which asserted that if Lyell applied his concept of natural laws operating on the surface of the earth he must apply them also to life, even to the human brain: if the earth had a history, so did its life forms. Chambers wrote: "It is hardly necessary to say, much less to argue, that mental action, being proved to be under law, passes at once into the category of natural things. Its old metaphysical character vanishes in a moment, and the distinction usually taken between physical and moral is annulled, as only an error in terms" (Chambers 331–32).

Throughout the period of these developments in science, the humanities retained to some extent the attitudes they had inherited through religion from Plato, Aristotle, the Neoplatonists, Saint Augustine, and medieval Christianity. The purpose of human existence was to know pure Being, or God himself: knowledge, therefore, was contemplation; "Reality" transcended the world of flux. The Romantic concept of aesthetic appreciation developed from this contemplative mode of knowing as the culture became more secular; and the literary work, reified by print literacy and differentiated from other discourse, therefore transcended the world of flux as well. The natural sciences had been undergoing, since Bacon, a transformation in their philosophy of knowledge from that of contemplation to that of practical experimentation, in which the test of knowledge was the ability to account for or elicit predictable changes (Dewey, *Reconstruction* 103–31).[2] But the humanities, occupied with the study of the culture's heritage of written texts, continued to locate truth in humanity's verbal expression, which since Plato tended to depict human nature as unchanging and truth as independent of matter. In the nineteenth century, literary study became more and more isolated in its aesthetic ideology, for it found itself at war not only with the natural sciences but also with the burgeoning social sciences.

While the empirical methods of science were revolutionizing geology and biology, they were also profoundly affecting the study of society. In 1776 Adam Smith presented the case for complete economic freedom, later called *laissez-faire* economics, in *The Wealth of Nations*. The utilitarian philosopher Jeremy Bentham proposed that society should strive to achieve the greatest good for the greatest number, for which reason individuals should be educated for general utility: utilitarians assumed the basis for human behavior to be self-interest. And Thomas Malthus attempted to demonstrate that because population increased geometrically and food supplies only arithmetically, human poverty was inevitable: only disease, war, famine, and "moral restraint" could avert catastrophic starvation. All three applied "natural" laws to the human population, thus providing in their own fields a version of the uniformitarianism that disturbed believers in a personal God. And all three ignored any spiritual component to the human being. Uniformitarianism, like democratic political philosophy, moved responsibility for the individual's survival from an external authority—in the social world, the state; and in the natural world, God—to the individual, whose intrinsic significance it simultaneously cast into doubt by its focus on the system of society, on the system of living organisms, or on geological time. Paradoxically, as the individual gained freedom in the late eighteenth and early nineteenth centuries, the individual became aware of the struggle for life that unsponsored existence implied: the individual lost the security that knowledge of his or her place in the Great Chain of Being had once provided.

The uniformitarianism in the sciences induced a naturalistic attitude to social phenomena in some philosophers, scholars, artists, and writers. In France, Auguste Comte published the six volumes of his *Course of Positive*

Philosophy (1830–42), in which he rejected both theological and metaphysical explanations of the world in favor of "positivism," which was based on scientifically verifiable truth; he established the discipline of "sociology" as the scientific study of society. Biblical scholars began to examine the Bible "positivistically," considering it as a historical text expressive of the time and place in which it was written whose stories about Creation and the Flood belonged to mythology. In 1842 Honoré de Balzac, in the preface to his *Human Comedy*, implicitly compared his task of writer to that of the zoologist: "There is but one Animal. The Creator works on a single model for every organized being. 'The Animal' is elementary, and takes its external form, or, to be accurate, the differences in its form, from the environment in which it is obliged to develop" (12). In 1849 Courbet painted *The Stone Breakers*, an unidealized representation of peasants, for which Courbet was condemned by a contemporary critic for wanting "to depict as crudely as possible that which is revoltingly foul and crude" (quoted in Foucart 19). In 1880, in *The Experimental Novel*, Emile Zola explained the relationship he saw between the novel and the science of his time:

> The experimental novel is a consequence of the scientific evolution of the century; it continues and completes physiology, which itself leans for support on chemistry and medicine; it substitutes for the study of the abstract and the metaphysical man the study of the natural man, governed by physical and chemical laws, and modified by the influences of his surroundings; it is in one word the literature of our scientific age, as the classical and Romantic literature corresponded to a scholastic and theological age. (Zola 651)

Even literary history of the period showed the influence of evolutionary theory, particularly that of Lamarck. The Frenchman Hippolyte Taine, in his *History of English Literature*, which he published between 1863 and 1867, argued that literature was a product of "the race, the surroundings, and the epoch" (607), that

> Man, forced to accommodate himself to circumstances, contracts a temperament and a character corresponding to them; and his character, like his temperament, is so much more stable, as the external impression is made upon him by more numerous repetitions, and is transmitted to his progeny by a more ancient descent. So that at any moment we may consider the character of a people as an abridgment of all its preceding actions and sensations. (608)

For Taine literary works merited study as documents of a nation's moral history in a given age, though the great poems and novels were "more instructive than a heap of historians with their histories" (613). Taine retained a distinction between literature and other forms of discourse, insisting, at the end of his introduction, that literary works were instructive for being beautiful, useful in accordance with their perfection, and documentary only because of being "monuments." The aim of literature was to represent sentiments, and "the more a book represents important sentiments, the higher is its place in literature" (614).

The evolutionism in the air in the late nineteenth century made its way into literary study in three ways: (1) the application of the principle of evolutionary change to literature, whereby literature appeared to develop in relation to society; (2) the consideration of the literary and social environment as a determining factor of artistic production; and (3) the conception of the literary scholar as a social scientist, as an analytical observer of literary texts rather than as an appreciator or an evaluator of the aesthetic nature of literature (Pizer, *Realism* 78–79). In the United States, Hamlin Garland completed in 1887 a history of American literature titled "The Evolution of American Thought" (never published), where he wrote, "Nothing is stable, nothing absolute, all changes, all is relative. Poetry, painting, the drama, these too are always being modified or left behind by the changes in society from which they spring" (quoted in Pizer, "Evolutionary Foundation" 92). Influenced by Taine, Garland believed that literature was inseparable from life, governed by the same natural laws that governed life, reflective of particular social conditions of a particular era; therefore, good fiction did not obey abstract aesthetic rules inherited from the past but instead represented faithfully contemporary human events (Pizer, *Realism* 69).

Thomas Sergeant Perry, who had become a reviewer of foreign literature for the *Atlantic Monthly* in 1869, wrote that although the idea that "something out of nothing by direct exercise of creative power . . . has vanished from science, it still survives in those departments of human activity which have not yet come fully under scientific treatment, and poets and painters enjoy in the popular estimation a privilege which has been denied to nature" (quoted in Pizer, *Realism* 83). Perry thus criticized the reverence for the literary text that Arnold had expressed. In their determinism these literary evolutionists (Garland, Perry, and William Dean Howells) denied to the author the importance that the Romantics, with their belief in genius, had bestowed upon the author, and they denied to the literary work its Romantic aura of aesthetic truth. In so doing they brought into the discipline the debate which, decades later, Rene Wellek and Austin Warren (Wellek and Warren, *Theory*)[3] would characterize as between intrinsic and extrinsic approaches to the text, the debate between the New Critics and the Marxist and Freudian critics in the early twentieth century.

The empiricism of geology, natural history, economics, and nineteenth-century naturalistic art and literature expressed the materialist approach to truth allowed by Cartesian dualism, as did Darwin's method of obtaining knowledge about evolution. But Darwin's theory of the mechanism whereby species evolved—natural selection—signaled early the ending of the dualist paradigm.[4] In coming to his conclusion of natural selection, Darwin combined his knowledge of artificial selection, an ordinary practice in England among stockbreeders and farmers, with Malthus's theory of the struggle for existence arising from the geometrical progression of the population rate. Natural selection meant that those individual organisms that fortuitously had developed novelties beneficial to their health would survive and would transmit genetically the advantages to their offspring; in geological time the accumulation of those genetic changes would lead to species change. *Laissez-faire* economics governed nature, where survival resulted from successful competition. No God intervened. The final paragraph of the *Origin of Species* indicated the reason for studying nature ecologically, as a system:

> It is interesting to contemplate a tangled bank, clothed with many plants of many kinds, with birds singing on the bushes, with various insects flitting about, and with worms crawling through the damp earth, and to reflect that these elaborately constructed forms, so different from each other, and dependent upon each other in so complex a manner, have all been produced by laws acting around us. (450).

In 1871 Darwin made explicit the implications of natural selection for mankind in *The Descent of Man*. As he wrote in its introduction, he had thought that readers would understand from his *Origin of Species* that "man must be included with other organic beings in any general conclusion respecting his manner of appearance on this earth" (1), but the public, including many scientists, had exempted man from such consideration in recognition of the potential religious implications to "the evolution of man." Louis Agassiz, professor of zoology and geology at the Lawrence Scientific School at Harvard at the time of its publication, who had argued in 1842 that the progressiveness of the fossil record proved that the "history of the earth proclaims its Creator" (quoted in Ruse 97),[5] opposed evolutionary theory to the day of his death in 1873. And Darwin's most vocal supporter among the scientists, Asa Gray, in 1860 wrote a lengthy, complimentary review of the *Origin* in the *American Journal of Science and Arts* in which he judged it probable "that our author [Darwin] regards the whole system of nature as one which had received at its first formation the impress of the will of its Author."[6] With the later book, Darwin offered scientific evidence for what Robert Chambers had asserted in 1844, that "mental action" belonged to the category of natural things and that therefore "the distinction between physical and moral is annulled." Thus Darwin showed the unity of soul and body, mind and matter. By the end of the eighties, scientists recognized the wide-reaching consequences of Darwin's discoveries. An article appearing in *Popular Science Monthly* indicated the extent to which the scientific ideas had reached the general public:

> Through enormous labors during the past thirty years the science of biology has covered the ground once supposed to be peculiarly the domain of mind, and the natural history of man, both body and mind, are so well known in their most general features that the biologists of every country are agreed that man is an evolved animal, that his lineage can be traced back into the geologic past and to an animal pedigree. In mind and body he has an ancestry reaching into time indefinitely remote, and those who hate to believe it are silenced by the evidence and no longer strive against it. Their only hope is to show reasonable grounds for the belief that Nature has in some way and at some time been supplemented, and that man has some arbitrary mental gifts that can not be deduced from his natural history. This acquired knowledge of the natural history of man has revolutionized every former conception of him, and has rendered worthless—absolutely worthless—almost everything that has been written. Not only physical science, but especially history, philosophy, psychology, ethics—all had to be rewritten, and all *educational institutions founded upon these, as most all have been*, have got to be metamorphosed to adapt them to the knowledge which has been acquired in this century and mostly within the last half of it. (Dolbear 755)

Darwin had removed the metaphysical foundation for the spirit/matter dualism. And in time the news of God's death "reached the ears of men" in fields other than biology. As the philosopher John Dewey wrote in 1910: "In laying hands upon the sacred ark of absolute permanency, in treating the forms that had been regarded as types of fixity and perfection as originating and passing away, the 'Origin of Species' introduced a mode of thinking that in the end was bound to transform the logic of knowledge, and hence the treatment of morals, politics, and religion" (*Influence* 1–2). Upon the scientific acceptance of the *Origin of Species* and *The Descent of Man*, by the end of the 1880s, the culture had begun a paradigm shift to a relativistic holism, to the ecological model of reality whereby things (organisms, events, and even the "self") were definable not by any apparently intrinsic ("God-given") meanings but rather by their function in systems. In the course of this shift the notion of an eternal order, whose permanent forms were endowed with intrinsic meaning, yielded to that of a world of flux.

"What a piece of work is a man!" says Hamlet. "How noble in reason! . . . in apprehension how like a god!" Although in Shakespeare's play his words are replete with irony, Hamlet gives the basic tenets of Renaissance humanism, those which Bacon enunciates without irony: "Man, if we look to final causes, may be regarded as the centre of the world; insomuch that if man were taken away from the world, the rest would seem to be all astray, without aim or purpose" (6: 747).

Because the discipline of literary study, when it took secular shape in the latter half of the nineteenth century, occupied itself with the appreciation and analysis of literary "masterpieces" (which did not include contemporary novels) and largely ignored advances in science, its proponents absorbed and promulgated the values implicit in such works as *Hamlet*. From long before science dwarfed the individual in the vastness of a universe which did not center on humanity, literature had expressed the emotional life of the individual. And after the publications of Buffon, Lamarck, Lyell, Chambers, and Darwin threatened to prove mankind an accident of nature's history, many professors of the liberal arts in American colleges and universities found refuge in the humanism of their subject matter, believing that the lesson of great literature lay in its depiction of an unchanging human spirit. Because the liberal arts dominated the curriculum of most institutions until the 1870s, that humanist philosophy dominated higher education and the college-educated elite.[7]

For many reasons the culture recoiled at Darwin's proposal of natural selection as the mechanism for evolutionary change. Since the fourth century B.C. Western civilization had held, simultaneously, and more or less consciously, both the Platonic belief that the sensible realm of earthly change was but a poor reflection of a superior intelligible realm of permanent Forms, and the Aristotelian belief that nature was ordered in a gradation, a ladder, from the inanimate to the animate, from plants to primitive organisms, to fish, reptiles, birds, and mammals, and then to human beings. Christianity had converted these assumptions into its model of the Great Chain of Being, whereby the human, composed of both spirit and matter, occupied a position lower than the angels but higher than the most intelligent mammals, midway between God and inanimate matter. Humanity could obtain Truth and salvation through revelation or could obtain damnation, as did Christopher Marlowe's sixteenth-century Dr. Faustus, for pursuing earthly knowledge to the neglect of the spirit. Since good—and therefore morality—was associated with spirit and evil with matter, to covet the material, whether knowledge or wealth, was a sin. For traditional nineteenth-century Christians who believed in the Great Chain of Being and refrained, as the Church demanded, from questioning God's ways, the empirical geologists and naturalists (even those who were clergymen) were engaged in a damnable interrogation of divinely ordained nature. Darwin challenged the belief in God in numerous ways: by presenting evidence that the natural order was not fixed, that the species were not permanent, that the human being had evolved in the course of millions of years from less complex organisms, that human consciousness was inseparable from material existence, and that the individual life depended not on God's decision but instead on the individual's occasionally fortuitous genetic fitness for the environment in a fierce competition for survival. "Natural selection" turned divine intervention into a myth.

Since for Western culture morality rested upon the independence of the human spirit from biological forces, Darwinism appeared to threaten the moral basis for civilization. So those late nineteenth-century American educators who believed that the purpose of education was to refine the individual's moral faculty attacked Darwinian science for its amorality. In 1871, the year Darwin published *The Descent of Man*, Noah Porter said in his Yale presidential inaugural address:

> We desire more instead of less Christianity in this university. We do not mean that we would have religion take the place of intellectual activity, for this would tend to dishonor Christianity itself by an ignorant and narrow perversion of its claims to supremacy. . . . But we desire that all science should be more distinctly connected with that thought and goodness which are everywhere manifested in the universe of matter and of spirit; that the scientific poverty of the atheistic materialism should be clearly proved to the understanding as well as felt to be repellant to the heart. . . . (Quoted in Veysey 45–46)

Twenty years later, in 1893, after Darwinism had converted natural history into modern biology, Jacob Gould Schurman, president of Cornell University, associated Darwinism with utilitarianism in *The Ethical Import of Darwinism*:

> Biology has led up to an ethical theory which places the governing principle of human conduct in utility; since, on its showing, utility has generated that conduct as well as the life and the species in which it is manifested. . . . Moral rules are regarded as the expression of those social adaptations which, on the whole, and after infinite gropings, proved most serviceable in the preservation of groups of human animals in the struggle for existence. . . .
>
> Does not the evolutionary doctrine of heredity imply that man is what his ancestry has made him, and so abrogate our belief in the freedom of the human will? And does not goodness cease to be divine when you have explained moral laws as a statement of the habits blindly struck out and blindly followed by simian or semi-human groups in the struggle for existence? . . .
>
> But besides mere life there is spirit, with its powers of apprehending the true, the good, and the beautiful. (123, 154, 183)

Because university presidents were selected not only for their academic qualifications but also for their philosophical positions regarding higher education, their views indicated the major issues of the intellectual life of the late nineteenth century. For Schurman, horrified by the Darwinian assertion that, in his words, "morality . . . had a mechanical origin" (141), the culture should distinguish between Darwin's observations of natural "facts" and Darwin's speculations on the origins of the moral faculty (181). Such a distinction between the study of the human spirit and the study of nature meant the continuation in the structure of higher education of the dualism of spirit and matter that biology itself had discredited.

The defenders of the liberal arts were fighting not only the biologists, however. American economists, among them Yale's William Graham Sumner, from the early seventies were applying Darwinian natural selection to society as an argument against government intervention in the marketplace. In "Social Darwinism," as this doctrine was called, the "survival of the fittest" (a slogan coined by Herbert Spencer, who had developed his social evolutionism in relation to Lamarck) justified the immense accumulation of wealth by such tycoons as John D. Rockefeller in the *laissez-faire* capitalism of the period. Spencer visited the United States in 1882 to publicize his two social principles: (1) "Every man has freedom to do all that he wills, provided he infringes not the equal freedom of any other man"; and (2) "Each individual ought to receive the benefits and evils of his own nature and consequent conduct, neither being prevented from having whatever good his actions normally bring to him, nor allowed to shoulder off on to other persons whatever ill is brought to him by his actions" (quoted in Boller 51).

Darwinian biology and Social Darwinism, both of which ignored "the human spirit" as irrelevant to the processes of natural and social change, focused on the individual only as a repository of self-centered biological drives geared toward personal survival. In the late nineteenth century, the social change accomplished by the interaction of individuals amassing their own fortunes went by the name of progress. These individuals Arnold would have called Philistines, and their increasing economic control of American life sent many humanist intellectuals back to Arnold's "sweetness and light" for a secular salvation from what they considered the evils of materialism. The discipline of literary study, which sought out works like *Hamlet* for their expression of the human condition, became the humanists' preserve. And the barriers literary scholars erected against the scientists' "atheist materialism" served also as barriers against a materialist society.

In the Renaissance, humanism was a revolutionary movement, presenting a human-centered orientation in the acquisition of knowledge rather than a God-centered one by focusing on the works of classical Greece and Rome rather than on the sacred Christian texts, but in the nineteenth century humanism occupied a different position in the culture. The divorce of the humanities from the sciences allowed the discipline of classical study, concerned with a limited body of texts, to retain more or less the same ideology from the seventeenth century through the nineteenth, regardless of what the sciences might be discovering about nature. In face of the increasing credibility of natural science in the 1870s, humanist scholars in America fought to continue the classical curriculum as a means to combat atheism, for the classical tradition idealized the human being, whose spiritual aspect these scholars did not question. In his 1870 book *The American Colleges and the American Public*, which he wrote before becoming Yale's president, Porter argued:

> Man and nature are alike the works of God. The science of each naturally leads us to God, but surely neither the mechanism of the masses of the universe, nor the chemistry of its molecules, nor the history of the development of its forces are *better* fitted to bring us any nearer to Him than the constitution and workings of the soul, with its manifestations in literature, and its developments in human history. . . .
> . . . Religious influences and religious teaching should be employed in colleges, in order to exclude and counteract the atheistic tendencies of much of modern science, literature, and culture" (65, 224).

Inheritors of the ideology of their subject matter, the classics professors believed that human nature had not changed since Homer and that therefore the classical texts instructed young men adequately in human conduct. Since for them truth about the world was a fixed quantum, and only worthwhile insofar as it concerned humanity, the curriculum that had educated men of letters since the seventeenth century should continue to do so. And they defended it with religious intensity. They recognized that if scientists achieved the "death of man"—that is, the loss of faith in the human being's God-given spirit—scientists would have achieved the "death of God." Civilization's morality was at stake.

Before the Civil War the curriculum of American men's colleges included mainly studies in Greek, Latin, mathematics, logic, and moral philosophy, with occasionally some Hebrew, elementary physics or astronomy, and natural history (Hofstadter 11). And although in general the women's colleges, or seminaries, tended to give more emphasis to the fine arts (Schmidt 141–142), the curriculum of the seminaries actually differed little from that of the colleges (Kelly 64, Ross 5). Greek and Latin grammar, considered difficult subjects, were supposed to discipline the mind and develop moral character,[8] serving well the purposes of the sectarian boards who dominated the prewar colleges. In the debate as to whether higher education should dedicate itself solely to the acquisition of mental and moral power or should also include the accumulation of knowledge ("the furnishing of the mind"), a debate that continued through the 1870s, humanists defended their discipline against science by deprecating the collection of scientific "facts" and by arguing that the actual practice of science required such intellectual training as was attainable by the study of language. Basically, the humanists did not recognize as serious scholarly endeavor the kind of field work naturalists did. In 1870 Porter wrote:

> We contend, moreover, that such a [scientific] training, if it were more uniformly successful in its results, would not as a discipline take the place of that which the study of language imparts and involves, for the reason that it neither requires so subtle a use of the intellect, nor one that is so manifold and various. The Physical sciences do indeed bring us in contact with *nature*, and invite us to discover or contemplate her laws. But Literary studies [of the classics] confront us with *man* as exhibited either in the refined relations of thought and feeling that have been inwrought into the structure of language, or in the expressions of thought and feeling that are enshrined by literature. They are properly and preeminently human and humanizing studies, inasmuch as they continually present man to us in the various workings of his higher nature. (64–65)

Within the humanities the battle between contemplative knowledge (the spiritual) and practical knowledge (the material) expressed itself in the classicists' opposition to the admission of modern languages and literatures, including English, into the curriculum. The proponents of the study of modern literature—that is, the literature of the modern languages—who objected to the uselessness of the traditional curriculum, had accepted the model of learning put forth first by the scientists whereby the purpose of education was the accumulation of a body of knowledge and an acquaintance with useful methods for investigating nature.[9] Having abandoned the educational philosophy that the analysis of Greek and Latin grammar instilled mental discipline in young men and thereby prepared them for the unexpected challenges of life, Harvard's president Charles William Eliot and others supporting the study of modern languages and literatures saw the study of classical texts as an apparent end in itself for its professors and of doubtful benefit to its nonacademic possessors. Aware that scientists needed German and French to keep abreast of scientific discoveries in Europe, they advocated relaxing the requirement of classical languages in the curriculum to allow the substitution of German and French: the German and French languages would serve scientists and social scientists as instruments to obtain knowledge, and the German and French literatures, as well as English literature, would serve humanists as subject matter. Eliot, who in an 1884 address titled "What Is a Liberal Education?" called for the addition of English language and literature, French and German, history, economics, and natural science to the liberal arts curriculum, said:

Without a knowledge of these two languages [French and German] it is impossible to get at the experience of the world upon any modern industrial, social, or financial question, or to master any profession which depends upon applications of modern science. I urge no utilitarian argument, but rest the claims of French and German for admission to complete academic equality on the copiousness and merit of the literatures, and the indispensableness of the languages to all scholars. (51)

The utilitarian argument for the inclusion of French and German into the curriculum benefited enthusiasts of the literature of "the mother tongue." Lafayette College had had America's first professor of the English language and comparative philology, Francis Andrew March, since 1857 (Parker, "Where Do English Departments Come From?" 345). In 1867 President Andrew Lipscomb of the University of Georgia instituted a course of study for students pursuing a scientific education that included English, French or German, and mathematics (Dyer 115). Harvard, which had offered modern foreign literature since 1819, when it made George Ticknor the Smith professor of French and Spanish literatures (P. Franklin 359), in 1876 designated Francis James Child, who had been teaching rhetoric, its first professor of English. It granted Child's student Robert Grant the first American Ph.D. in English literature the same year (Applebee 27). President Eliot said, "I recognize but one mental acquisition as an essential part of the education of a lady or a gentleman—namely, an accurate and refined use of the mother-tongue" (quoted in Shipman 145). And Paul R. Shipman, in an 1880 article in *The Popular Science Monthly*, wrote, "Our mother-tongue alone, as the instrument of our thinking, is the instrument of our culture," to be studied through "the best writers and speakers of the tongue" (Shipman 149). The textbook that Child used at Harvard, George Marsh's *The Origin and History of the English Language and of the Early Literature It Embodies*, published in 1862, contributed to the inseparability of modern language and literary study as well as to the definition of the discipline: a philologist, Marsh argued for the study of language in a literary context, set up a series of literary periods into which literature could be divided, and showed how literature could be related to national character (P. Franklin 360–61).

In 1883 A. Marshall Elliott with two colleagues established the Modern Language Association of America in a meeting at Columbia College, where they held its first convention: forty teachers from at least twenty-two institutions attended (Parker, "The MLA" 3–4). The group passed the following resolution: "That, in the opinion of the Association, the chief aims to be sought in the study of modern languages in our colleges are literary culture, philological scholarship, and linguistic discipline, but that a course in oral practice is desirable as an auxiliary" (quoted in Parker, "The MLA" 20).

The triumph of modern literary study was not a victory for utilitarianism, because professors of the new, enlarged discipline—which included classical languages and literatures, modern foreign languages and literatures, and English language and literature—inherited the ideology of the classicists: that literary studies, in Porter's words, "are properly and preeminently human and humanizing studies, inasmuch as they continually present man to us in the various workings of his higher nature." As science won prestige and authority, and as business and industry expanded in the late nineteenth-century *laissez-faire* economy (producing, in the eyes of Arnoldian humanists, Philistinism), the discipline of literary study interpreted the expression of that "higher nature."

The isolation of the discipline of literary study came about as a result of the confluence of many ideas: the Aristotelian notion that poetry was "higher" than history; the Baconian distinction between poesy and science, which turned literature into spiritual nourishment; the Arnoldian conviction that literature, "by means of its spiritual standard of perfection," enabled its readers to escape Philistinism; specialization; "academic freedom"; the land-grant movement, which gave rise to the concept of democratic education; and the discipline's acceptance of Cartesian reductionism in its teaching and research practices.

The idealized social distance between the university and the political world was simultaneously challenged by the elective system and buttressed by the concept of academic freedom. With his goal of freedom in all areas of intellectual endeavor, Eliot promoted in his 1869 inaugural address the elective system, for which Harvard gained a temporary notoriety. In 1872 Harvard abolished all requirements for particular courses for seniors; in 1879 for juniors; in 1884 for sophomores; and in 1895 for freshmen, except for English and a foreign language. Appropriate for a democratic country, according to Eliot, the elective system transformed the higher education that had been the province of the wealthy, with its prescribed program of the "useless" liberal arts, into a pluralistic offering of academic disciplines that enabled young men (but not young women) of various classes to obtain the intellectual skills they desired for a career. The elective system conformed to the *laissez-faire* capitalist principle of the division of labor—intellectual labor—and thus contributed both to social mobility and to the increasing economic efficiency of late nineteenth-century America by encouraging specialization (Hofstadter 49–51).

Opponents of the elective system feared not only the intrusion of nongentlemen into the university but also the loss of spiritual value to the curriculum: they had defended the liberal arts education for its function of mental and spiritual discipline, which the "sin-sick soul" needed (Phillips 214), and they recognized quickly the utilitarianism of the new pedagogical philosophy. For them the elective system had brought about a trivialization of education, a lowering of standards, and an excessive vocationalism; it had brought about as well a disintegration of the community of the educated, who under the traditional system had shared attitudes and values acquired by studying the liberal arts, the attitudes and values of their class (Hofstadter 53–56). It had undermined the vertical social hierarchy still functioning in America. Irving Babbitt wrote in 1908, regarding its implications, "Even if we sacrifice the letter of the old Bachelor of Arts degree, we should strive to preserve its spirit. This spirit is threatened at present in manifold ways,—by the upward push of utilitarianism and kindergarten methods, by the downward push of professionalism and specialization, by the almost irresistible pressure of commercial and industrial influences" (115–16). By accommodating the particular material needs of students, free election of courses signified the secularization of higher education: higher education served no longer the individual's soul but rather the individual's social and material well-being in a world that required for its economic and technological growth experts trained in innumerable fields. Authoritarian education had yielded to democratic education.

The elective system, combined with society's increasing professionalism in the late nineteenth century, effected the division of professors into disciplinary departments, where professors concentrated on research and teaching within the areas of their greatest interest. With the assumption that specialization served the nonscientific disciplines as well as it did the scientific, when higher education gave science an important position in the curriculum in the latter half of the nineteenth century it implemented specialization in all disciplines. Furthermore, the intent of the universities to offer graduate education of the quality available in Germany, coupled with the competition among universities for prestige, made specialization imperative: competition entailed publication, and publication seemed to require mastery of a narrow field. *Specialist* came to indicate competence, and *dilettante* became a word of scorn.[10]

The combination of the elective system and academic specialization affected not only the disciplines themselves and the relationship between disciplines but also the relationship of the university to society. In the next hundred years the university would become more than a place for the preservation and advancement of knowledge; by affiliating itself with government and industry in military and technological research, it would become a force for social change. Yet within the academy most humanists eschewed involvement with politics, industry, and science, and thus positioned themselves on the margins of public interest.

That disdain for the material, which made the discipline of literary study a supporter of the political status quo, characterized most of the young scholars entering the profession in the late nineteenth and early twentieth century. The spirit/matter battles—those taking place between the classicists and the modernists, those between the humanists and the scientists, those between the "pure" scientists and the technologists, and those between the university and society—were to some extent battles of social class, as became evident in the debate over the aims of higher education carried by such periodicals as *Popular Science Monthly*. The traditional liberal arts education was for gentlemen (not ladies, and not laborers) and was valued by gentlemen precisely because it could not serve material ends. As Edward Youmans, editor of *Popular Science Monthly*, observed in 1872,

> To the popular indictment that classical studies are not "practical" they [the defenders of the classics] have pleaded guilty, but have claimed that this alleged vice is in reality a virtue. The whole literature of that side of the question has been pervaded by a scorn of utility, and a contempt for the "practical." The dead languages have been advocated, not for their ulterior uses, but as mental gymnastics in which discipline of the faculties is the object to be obtained. It has not been denied that the sciences were "practical," but practical ends have themselves been repudiated as low, sordid, and unworthy. (625)

Through the end of the nineteenth century generally those who had gone to the expensive prep schools continued to choose the classical education, in which they studied literature, over the scientific education, whereas those who viewed higher education as a means to improve their social standing studied other, more "useful" subjects, such as science.[11] Enthusiasts of science had even argued for its inclusion in the curriculum on the basis of its democratic character, as did Denison Olmsted in an 1855 article in *Barnard's Journal of Education*:

> Science, in its very nature, tends to promote political equality; to elevate the masses; to break down the spirit of aristocracy; and to abolish all those artificial distinctions in society which depend on differences of dress, equipage, style of living, and manners; to raise the industrial classes to a level with the professional; and to bring the country, in social rank and respectability, to a level with the city. (Quoted in Hughes 144)

Contending that a democracy was obliged to provide education for all, even women, various intellectuals began arguing in the 1870s for a modification of the aims of higher education, to which end William P. Atkinson of the Massachusetts Institute of Technology wrote in *Popular Science Monthly* that a major influence on education was the

> first real attempt to combine republican ideas with the theory of liberal education—in other words, to make the education of the whole people liberal, instead of merely the education of certain privileged classes and protected professions. And when I say the whole people, I mean *men and women*. Nothing, I will say in passing, to my mind so marks us as still educational barbarians, so stamps all our boasted culture with illiberality, as an exclusion of the other sex from all share in its privileges. (2)

Public enthusiasm for democracy did not strengthen the humanities. Advocates of literary study in the late nineteenth century found the discipline marginalized not only by science but also by professional schools, which appealed to a public increasingly concerned that the university be a service institution. In the 1850s, when a committee appointed by the Board of Trustees of the University of Georgia was preparing a proposal to the state legislature to revamp the university to include among its offerings the study not only of the modern languages but also of agriculture, "applied sciences," teacher education, and law, the young scientist Joseph LeConte argued that "the utilitarian spirit, like a dreadful vampire, is sucking the blood of our spiritual life" (quoted in Dyer 89); the proposal failed. But after the Civil War enthusiasm increased in the South as well as elsewhere for providing practical education. The Morrill Act of 1862 (modified in 1866 to include the Confederate states) granted large tracts of federal land to states that would provide for agricultural and mechanical instruction at the college level; and by defining the public university in terms of its responsibility to serve the practical needs of the state, it led universities to include under their auspices colleges of business and law as well as agriculture and engineering. The Georgia legislature accepted Morrill funds in 1872. Thus the Morrill Act and the elective system in combination converted the "university" into the modern "multiversity."

By the 1890s, "democracy in education" had come to be associated with "reality," a term used to indicate the practical aspects of human life. Democratic education took on a variety of meanings: equality of all fields of learning; equality of treatment for all students attending a university; accessibility of the institution to a variety of students (including women, members of minority groups, and those with poor preparatory backgrounds); the abandonment of the classical language requirement; the offering of technical training within the university (for those students eager to succeed in "the real world"); the dissemination of skills in agriculture and engineering; and even the assumption that the state university should be governed by the nonacademic public, that it had a popular mandate (Veysey 61–65). In 1907 President Andrew S. Draper of the University of Illinois, a land-grant university, declared: "The universities that would thrive must put away all exclusiveness and dedicate themselves to universal public service. They must not try to keep people out; they must help all who are worthy to get in" (40). Arguing that the American university would "carry the benefits of scientific research to the doors of the multitude" (41), Draper relegated the humanities to the "literary colleges," which would "flourish so long as, and wherever, they can provide the best instruction in the humanities," and these colleges would "train for culture" (40). For the utilitarian Draper, training for culture was less important than bringing the benefits of science to the people. The effect of such "democracy," the effect of the transformation of universities into clusters of technical schools offering vocational training to those seeking to better their social status through material success, was to render the discipline of literary study more and more vulnerable to attack for its apparent uselessness.

Draper's model of the modern university, or "multiversity," encountered opposition from scholars who continued to believe that the purpose of university education should be the disinterested pursuit of knowledge. Veblen expressed outrage in 1918 that universities were neglecting "higher" learning:

> The greater number of these state schools are not, or are not yet, universities except in name. These establishments have been founded, commonly, with a professed utilitarian purpose, and have started out with professional training as their chief avowed aim. The purpose made most of in their establishment has commonly been to train young men for proficiency in some gainful occupation. (43)

For Veblen, a college of commerce, "the perfect flower of the secularization of the universities" (205), was particularly out of place in an institution of higher learning: its purpose was to enhance individual gain at the cost of the community at large, and so it was "peculiarly incompatible with the collective cultural purpose of the university" (209–10). Business schools and law schools, Veblen argued in *The Higher Learning in America*, did not serve well a democracy; they served the interests of one class against another (212). By encouraging young men to take interest in their own prospective material success, the elective system effectively decreased the importance of all courses whose content was not immediately useful; and by including professional schools in universities the Morrill Act, in its effect, bestowed academic prestige on vocational training.

For President Clark Kerr of the University of California, speaking at Harvard in 1963, the elective system in the long run benefited more the professors than the students: "Freedom for the student to choose became freedom for the professor to invent; and the professor's love of specialization [became] the students' hate of fragmentation" (14–15). The twentieth-century multiversity had become only "a name": "It is not one community but several—the community of the undergraduate and the community of the graduate; the community of the humanist, the community of the social scientist, and the community of the scientist; the communities of the professional schools; the community of all the nonacademic personnel; the community of the administrators" (18–19). The name of the institution stood not for a faculty unified in purpose but instead for "a certain standard of performance, a certain degree of respect, a certain historical legacy, a characteristic quality of spirit" (19).

In the 1980s higher education has become a subject of intense scrutiny; and at the same time that the multiversity is attracting more monies from industry and the government than ever before, more and more thinkers are criticizing the practices of early specialization and vocational training and are calling for a revaluation of the liberal arts. In *The University and the Public Interest*, published in 1981, President A. Bartlett Giamatti of Yale laments the vocationalism "that strangles the power of choice in the name of necessity and cripples the urge to a flexible civic sense when that sense ought to be gathering soundness and strength" (10). For Giamatti, "it is precisely now that the values, and value, of a liberal education must be asserted again, a liberal education whose intellectual core is a required curriculum and whose purpose is the development of students who can make rational, humane, informed choices, and citizens" (11).

Academic specialization, by linking professorial competence to expertise in narrowly defined fields of interest, had underpinned "academic freedom" at the end of the nineteenth century. The battle that scientists had to fight against the sectarian boards of American colleges and universities in the decade following Darwin's publication of the *Origin of Species* clarified the necessity for scholars to be free to pursue truth regardless of its implications for established values. American scholars adopted the concept of academic freedom from Germany, where, they learned in 1878, the university identified itself with the "ardent, methodical, independent search after truth in any and all its forms, but wholly irrespective of utilitarian applications" (quoted in Metzger 376). German scholars did not engage in politics, devoted as they were to scientific research, in a world that reflected the Kantian dichotomy between the realm of free will and that of causal necessity (390–91). American scientists, following the model of the German Ph.D., with its specialized dissertation of original research, learned to justify their teaching and their publication of texts that undermined society's cherished beliefs by pointing to their expertise in fields of learning with which the public was not familiar: at the frontiers of their respective disciplines experts could see things that the general public could not. Their responsibility to do research—to make new knowledge—and their responsibility to train graduate students to do research required an independence from political groups that might wish to repress theories or discoveries dangerous to the status quo. Furthermore, scientists in both Germany and the United States had learned that truth was tentative, to be sought through discussion that included disagreement, which only a climate of complete intellectual freedom could foster.

Eliot had broached the subject in his inaugural address: "The very word 'education' is a standing protest against dogmatic teaching. The notion that education consists in the authoritative inculcation of what the teacher deems true may be logical and appropriate in a convent, or a seminary for priests, but it is intolerable in universities and public schools, from primary to professional" (7–8). Years later, in an address he gave in 1898 called "The Aims of the Higher Education," Eliot said, "a university stands for intellectual and spiritual domination—for the forces of the mind and soul against the overwhelming load of material possessions, interest, and activities which the modern world carries" (92–93).

Academic "freedom," however, also carried responsibilities and restrictions. With the responsibility to communicate to students "the whole body of thought which has been accumulated in the department of knowledge in which he works" (Small 465), the scholar enjoyed freedom from public pressure only within that "department of knowledge." As President William R. Harper of the University of Chicago pointed out in 1900, in a general summary of the application of the principle in the last decades of the nineteenth century,

(1) A professor is guilty of an abuse of privilege who promulgates as truth ideas or opinions which have not been tested scientifically by his colleagues in the same department of research or investigation. (2) A professor abuses his privilege who takes advantage of a classroom exercise to propagate the partisan view of one or another of the political parties. (3) A professor abuses his privilege who in any way seeks to influence his pupils or the public by sensational methods. (4) A professor abuses his privilege of expression of opinion when, altho a student and perhaps an authority in one department or group of departments, he undertakes to speak authoritatively on subjects which have no relationship to the department in which he was appointed to give instruction. (5) A professor abuses his privilege in many cases when, altho shut off in large measure from the world and engaged within a narrow field of investigation, he undertakes to instruct his colleagues or the public concerning matters in the world at large in connection with which he has had little or no experience. (Quoted in Dewey, "Academic Freedom" 8–9)

Harper's discussion of academic freedom revealed the Cartesianism that supported it: that "truth" was distinct from political "partisan views"; that an external reality was divisible into "fields of investigation" that might have no relation to each other; that scholarship or scientific investigation within a narrow field gave little knowledge of the practical "world at large." Thus the concept of academic freedom, which allowed professors to present in the name of truth controversial discoveries and theories to a public afraid of challenges to their beliefs, functioned to reinforce both the disciplinary boundaries and the perceived dualist distinction between society's intellectual life and its political life. Furthermore, it justified academic specialization in all disciplines, because specialization granted to the academic the authority to speak on a topic.

Late to the dualist paradigm in part because of their lack of familiarity with science, humanities scholars resisted adopting the scientists' reductionist practice of partitioning reality for exploration. But under the influence of the scientists, literature professors delineated "fields of study," objects on which to focus; and, under pressure to compete with the scientists for graduate students, they offered philology as a specialization of sufficient difficulty to merit the Ph.D. By the end of the nineteenth century professors of literature had mapped out a literary terrain of periods, genres, major texts, and great figures to serve as an appropriate body of material for empirical examination. Once these scholars had such fields of study, they invested them with a value that would justify their professional attention to them: they had to do so, for they were part of an academic enterprise which demanded that each discipline have its own territory and that its scholars engage in research. Yet by dissociating literary texts from other texts as having spiritual value in a material world, and by defining their own activity of literary interpretation as distinct from and superior to more utilitarian occupations, professors of literature were isolating themselves from the rest of society and even from other academic disciplines. When higher education abandoned the philosophy of mental discipline as a preparation for involvement in public life in favor of the philosophy of the accumulation of specific knowledge for specific purposes, the humanities lost authority in the curriculum to the technological sciences, which could serve better society's material welfare, as could the professional schools.

Society's eventual acceptance of the principle of academic freedom, a concept applied to the humanities and social sciences as well as to the sciences, reinforced the separation of the discipline from the public. Founded upon the difference between, in President Eliot's words, "the forces of the mind and soul" and the forces of the material world, the principle of academic freedom tended to suppress faculty discussion of political matters outside the areas of their expertise. For professors of literature, who generally believed, since Kant, that "aesthetic" qualities were distinguishable from political arguments in a literary text, "academic freedom" reduced the range of their possible discourse to nonpolitical commentary on literary matters. In an age of specialists, humanist scholars of literature turned over to politicians the responsibility for commentary on public matters.

In his opposition of man and nature, Yale's President Porter revealed the grounds for the disjunction between the humanists and the scientists, between, in effect, the human-centered paradigm that governed literary scholarship well into the twentieth century and the emerging systems paradigm that shaped biology from the 1880s, expressed itself in avant-garde art and literature at the turn of the century, and restructured physics after 1905, the year of Einstein's Special Theory of Relativity. For the humanists any search for knowledge that did not contribute to an understanding of the human being's "higher nature" was of only peripheral value to education; and their constitution of a canon of humanity-oriented literary works, such as *Hamlet*, for their field of study sustained their repugnance for empirical science. Since Bacon had distinguished the humanist enterprise from the scientific, humanists had generally considered the discoveries of science irrelevant to their appreciation of great writing. Yet physicists and geologists were gradually discovering a universe vast in time and space, which seemed less and less to center on human beings; and biologists were gradually uncovering a nature "red in tooth and claw" (in Thomas Huxley's words), in which humanity constituted but one species among many, all struggling for survival in an unsponsored, unplanned, earth-wide ecosystem. And to them the notion of a human spirit residing in a body was archaic, a "poetic" myth.

The scientists' rejection of religious dogma in favor of a critical appraisal of established cultural beliefs required the practical separation of the university from society. But in the early twentieth century, while humanists were adopting the reductionist model for academic learning, scientists were moving the culture into a holism in which all things would seem connected: self and world, mind and body, culture and nature, and university and society.

In the course of a hundred years Cardinal Newman's university has become a nostalgic fiction, for technology has rendered illusory any separation of the academy from the capitalist culture supporting it. Now universities are competing with each other for industrial grants, particularly in the burgeoning field of biotechnology: Washington University at St. Louis has obtained a five-year, $23.5 million grant from Monsanto, and Harvard Medical School has obtained a ten-year, $70 million grant from the Hoechst firm of West Germany. The independence of scholars and scientists from the public, which served as the foundation of and justification for academic freedom, has given way to a holistic interaction of professor-scientist-entrepreneurs, industries, and the federal government; and the public—in the case of genetic engineering, in particular—is asking for a voice in biotechnological decisions. Moreover, it is not only business that has captured segments of the university for its own purposes; in 1984 the Department of Defense sponsored more than thirty research projects involving recombinant-DNA techniques at twenty-five major universities. Leon Wofsy, professor of microbiology and immunology at the University of California, Berkeley, in an article published in the *Journal of Higher Education*, asks: "Just what and how much must be left to the marketplace? Our priorities as a society? Our values as educators?" (490).

Literary critics in the first half of our century, especially those calling themselves the "New Critics," resisted technology's intrusion into higher education as Newman and Arnold had earlier resisted science's intrusion, and they intentionally ignored the implications for the discipline of literary study of the conversion of the university into the multiversity. Now that the Department of Defense and biotechnological corporations have forced upon scholars of all disciplines a recognition of the inextricability of the academy from the social-industrial world, now that literary theorists have acknowledged political values in our own discipline, now that not only philosophy and science but also business and the federal government have exploded the belief in a spirit/matter dualism, we humanists will have to redefine our purposes.

4

Dualism and the Canon

Tradition . . . cannot be inherited, and if you want it you must obtain it by great labour. It involves, in the first place, the historical sense, which we may call nearly indispensable to anyone who would continue to be a poet beyond his twenty-fifth year; and the historical sense involves a perception, not only of the pastness of the past, but of its presence; the historical sense compels a man to write not merely with his own generation in his bones, but with a feeling that the whole of the literature of Europe from Homer and within it the whole of the literature of his own country has a simultaneous existence and composes a simultaneous order.

—T. S. Eliot, *Sacred Wood*

That is it. Intellectual freedom depends upon material things. Poetry depends upon intellectual freedom. And women have always been poor, not for two hundred years merely, but from the beginning of time.

—Virginia Woolf, *A Room of One's Own*

In the early years of the twentieth century science seemed destined to acquire the power to explain not only the movements of galaxies and the emergence of species but also the functioning of the human brain. Psychology had taken from Darwin explanations for instinct, intelligence, and emotion, as well as for the evolution of mind (Angell 154), and sociology had applied Darwin's natural selection to society in Spencer's doctrine of the "survival of the fittest": both disciplines grounded their theories about human phenomena in science. Freud offered scientific evidence for his division of the human psyche into id, ego, and super ego. And although Marxism, which gained strength in the last decade of the nineteenth century in opposition to capitalism, did not embrace any connection between social and biological determinism, it too offered an all-encompassing theory for social change and human behavior.

These materialist views, which left little space for God and even less for the human spirit, differed fundamentally from those of T. S. Eliot, who had inherited from Shelley, Arnold, and Bradley a belief in the possibility of genius rising above events to reveal universal values and to provide insight into human nature. As the spirit/matter dualism approached its end, various competing monistic systems came out of the sciences and social sciences to supplant it, threatening the discipline of literary study with irrelevance. In the seventeenth and eighteenth centuries, when both scientists and humanists recognized a Cartesian reality of spirit and matter, both could accept the humanities as a legitimate exploration of the distinctly human aspect of reality; science investigated only matter. But when science began to question the assumption of "spirit," as did Darwin, and offer materialist explanations of even the human conscience, then it put literature on the defensive for its apparent uselessness and its lack of encyclopedic power to explain rationally the increasingly vast universe. For in the capitalism of late nineteenth- and early twentieth-century America, the public appreciated the apparent rationality of science for its economic efficiency more than it did the fantasy of literature: capitalists located truth in material knowledge. Eliot's early twentieth-century definition of literature as a body of works composed by geniuses capable of escaping their daily concerns to engage in higher discourse, followed by the New Critics' isolation of the individual work from its material context, represented the dualist paradigm's final defense of the spirit.

From the time that literature had become a definable category of text, texts had achieved literary status by the willingness of scholars to comment upon them as intrinsically interesting. For the New Critics, whose original core was a group of American professors of literature associated with the South in the 1930s,[1] the discipline of literary study rested upon the distinction of literary texts from others whose purpose was legal, propagandistic, historical, scientific, or technological and upon the distinction of literary commentary from history. As Allen Tate wrote in a 1940 essay titled "The Present Function of Criticism," critics should preserve "the belief, philosophically tenable, in a radical discontinuity between the physical and the spiritual realms" in order to elevate literary works above political discussion and thus to protect literature from censorship:

> The function of criticism should have been, in our time, as in all times, to maintain and to demonstrate the special, unique, and complete knowledge which the great forms of literature afford us. And I mean quite simply *knowledge*, not historical documentation and information. But our literary critics have been obsessed by politics, and when they have been convinced of the social determinism of literature, they have been in principle indistinguishable from the academic scholars,

who have demonstrated that literature does not exist, that it is merely history, which must be studied as history is studied, through certain scientific analogies. The scholars have not maintained the tradition of literature as a form of knowledge; by looking at it as merely one among many forms of social and political expression, they will have no defense against the censors of the power state, or against the hidden censors of the pressure group. (8)

However, for Virginia Woolf that radical discontinuity between the spiritual and the physical, or between literature and politics, was untenable, because it had supported for centuries the cultural illusion that the values of those in power were universal, to the disadvantage of women. Her observation of the dependence of intellectual freedom on material things, in *A Room of One's Own* (1929), signaled not only the end of the concept of literature as a discourse worthy of study for its aesthetic or philosophical content alone but also the end of the illusion that the discipline of literary study was itself free of ideology. With that book she heralded an investigation into the ideology of the discipline, the ideology of the canon, and the ideology of the dualist paradigm that supported it, setting an agenda for the feminist attack on the profession.

In reifying "reality," print literacy reified words, giving them apparent autonomy from their original contexts. In time the special organizations of words that presumably served no utilitarian purpose became—for literary scholars—"literary works," born of the imaginations of their authors with their meaning bestowed on them at their birth. The work's meaning, its content, hidden within the verbal form, became an object of search—a sacred treasure—for all the scholars and critics who believed in the transcendence of art over ordinary life. When the study of modern literature entered the academy, literary scholars began measuring the preciousness of that meaning not only by its transcendent "truth" value but also by the difficulty of the recovery process. As Roland Barthes wrote, the reign of the "Author" was necessarily the reign of the "Critic," for the belief in the author as an originator of valuable ideas generated the activity of deciphering the author's work (*Image* 147).[2]

The Romantic belief in the category of the aesthetic gave literary works their status of "icons" (Wimsatt) or "monuments" (T. S. Eliot), verbal artifacts detachable not only from politics and history but also, after Bradley, from morality. The reification of the poem, once closer to song than to artifact, removed it from its original context, from the social world of politics, economic need, and human relationships, to a transcendent realm where it could speak to the soul, or to the faculty of aesthetic judgment. This realm became "the tradition" for T. S. Eliot, who, in his 1917 essay "Tradition and the Individual Talent," modified Arnold's concept of "culture," which included nonliterary texts, to "the whole of the literature of Europe from Homer and within it the whole of the literature of [the writer's] own country" and then evaluated writers according to their participation in the tradition. Eliot's metaphorical description of the tradition revealed his notion of the literary artwork as a thing, though it revealed as well a relativism in that the artwork's meaning depended upon its relationship to the other monuments in the "ideal order":

> The existing monuments form an ideal order among themselves, which is modified by the introduction of the new (the really new) work of art among them. The existing order is complete before the new work arrives; for order to persist after the supervention of novelty, the *whole* existing order must be, if ever so slightly, altered; and so the relations, proportions, values of each work of art toward the whole are readjusted; and this is conformity between the old and the new. (50)

The meanings of the works depended, in Eliot's view, upon their relationship with the other literary works sanctified by the culture's educated for admission into the ideal order.

To enter that ideal order the writer needed a "historical sense," a perception "not only of the pastness of the past but of its presence," a sense "of the timeless as well as of the temporal and of the timeless and the temporal together," and an awareness that "he must inevitably be judged by the standards of the past" (50). The great writer possessed in addition the ability to exclude from poetry even his (or her) own personality: "Poetry is not a turning loose of emotion, but an escape from emotion; it is not the expression of personality, but an escape from personality" (58). And "the more perfect the artist, the more completely separate in him will be the man who suffers and the mind which creates" (54). Thus the great writer, according to Eliot, left behind the problems of immediate circumstances to engage in a dialogue with the past in the timeless tradition.

Eliot carried Arnold's antipathy for Philistinism into the twentieth century and passed it on to the American New Critics, setting up literature in opposition to bourgeois materialism and setting up the literary work in opposition to the personal, social, or political utterance. In so doing he established requirements for entry into the canon, requirements that functioned to exclude works by writers who did not participate in a dialogue with the established monuments—works that expressed anger at particular social injustices, that voiced personal pain, that described nonuniversal problems, works written by women, blacks, Native Americans, and others who chose to use the power of words to try to effect social change.

America's New Critics followed Bradley in their belief that poetry, or literature, deserved study for its aesthetic character rather than for its possible moral value; in rebellion against philological, historical, biographical, moralistic, and sociological approaches to literature, they argued for interpreting the literary work itself. John Crowe Ransom, in 1938, distinguished between literary critics and the New Humanists, led by Babbitt, who were, according to Ransom, "historians and advocates of a certain moral system" (332), and between literary critics and the Leftists, or Proletarians, who like the Humanists diverted attention from the aesthetic object to class consciousness. For Tate, the historical approach, with its varieties of social determinism, had undermined the tradition of literature as a distinct form of knowledge, the outcome of which might be the censorship of literature for its political expression: to save literature from suppression by "the power state," professors must maintain its status as a unique discourse offering "the only complete, and thus the most responsible, versions of our experience" (Tate 8, 4). For Ransom, the "object of a proper society is to instruct its members how to transform instinctive experience into aesthetic experience" (Ransom 42), and literature served this purpose, when the literary work itself was understood. The time had come for English departments to turn away from such activities as appreciation, discussion of the artwork's effect on the reader, synopsis and paraphrase of the poem, historical studies, linguistic studies, moral studies, and other "special studies which deal with some abstract or prose content taken out of the work" (Ransom 342–45) and instead teach literature "critically." Departments of economics, chemistry, sociology, theology, and architecture trained students in criticism of performance, and so should English (Ransom 337), in order to make the discipline more "scientific" (Ransom 329).

In 1938, Cleanth Brooks and Robert Penn Warren issued their textbook *Understanding Poetry*, whose opening "Letter to the Teacher" listed their three principles for studying a poem:

1. Emphasis should be kept on the poem as a poem.

2. The treatment should be concrete and inductive.

3. A poem should always be treated as an organic system of relationships, and the poetic quality should never be understood as inhering in one or more factors taken in isolation. (ix)

An analysis of a poem, according to Brooks and Warren, should therefore be a discussion of "the poet's adaptation of his means to his ends . . . of the relations of the various aspects of a poem to each other and to the total communication intended" (ix).

René Wellek and Austin Warren, in *Theory of Literature*, differentiated literary from scientific language (as Bacon had done over three centuries earlier) for being connotative rather than denotative, for being expressive, ambiguous, symbolic, occasionally nonreferential, and concerned with meter, alliteration, and patterns of sound (22–23). In 1946 W. K. Wimsatt and Monroe Beardsley published in the *Sewanee Review* "The Affective Fallacy" and "The Intentional Fallacy," which defined as fallacies for literary analysis the consideration of either the poet's intention or the poem's apparent psychological effects on the reader. "The outcome of either Fallacy, the Intentional or the Affective, is that the poem itself, as an object of specifically critical judgment, tends to disappear" (Wimsatt 21). A year later Brooks warned against paraphrase in "The Heresy of Paraphrase" (192–214), because, he showed, meaning could not be abstracted from language, content could not be abstracted from form.

Ransom, Tate, Brooks, Robert Penn Warren, Wimsatt, Beardsley, Wellek, Austin Warren, and others, in giving the discipline some of the purposes and expectations of empiricism—the disengagement of the object of interest from its context for close examination, and, with the ignoring of intention or effect, objectivity—gave both method and theory to young scholars exasperated with "curators" of literature (in Ransom's characterization of the appreciation school). They thereby made the discipline appear more rigorous, objective, and academically respectable. Print literacy and its accompanying dualism, by separating self from world, separated critic from work, setting the work in an "atmosphere" of its own, to be considered independently of authorial intention, effect, historical causes, or political implications.

New Criticism installed the Brooks-and-Warren canon in more than one generation of literary critics, for by making criticism of great literature the primary purpose for advanced literary study and by deprecating historical investigation as only accessory to the analysis of the individual work, the New Critial method discouraged the kind of cultural study that would produce either radical canon revision or a critique of the values implicit in canonization. It encouraged only the kind of canon revision that involved the canonization of previously undiscovered works that met New Critical standards. Just as Cartesian dualism had externalized reality, giving the scientists the illusion that nature was "out there," describable in neutral "ordinary" language, Cartesian dualism objectified "great literature" as somehow already determined by time. New Criticism placed the individual critic in the position of servant to the great work, and the critic's value, to the profession and to the students, depended upon the critic's ability to prove the greatness of the work. The notion that paraphrase was "heresy" served to preserve the work's aura of greatness (and of mystery) at the same time that it made the critic's task appear more difficult. Specialists in literature served their own interests as well by preserving the separateness of a literary canon from other social discourse; they could hardly do otherwise for they generally believed themselves incapable of speaking or writing authoritatively on matters outside their discipline, being specialists in literature alone. New Criticism thus established for the discipline a concrete body of material for study, a systematic (apparently objective and hence "scientific") methodology, and a means to evaluate scholarly research, as well as limits to the range of texts and approaches pertinent to the discipline.

The enormous success of the textbook *Understanding Poetry* owed itself not only to the excellence of Brooks's and Warren's own discussions of the poems but also to the practicality of the pedagogical technique: in the classroom the method allowed for professor and students together to learn to read a text closely, for its symbolism, its ironies, its tensions, its ambiguities. This appealed both to students impatient with the authoritarian practices accompanying the other approaches and to young professors eager to democratize the classroom. Since teachers trained in New Critical methodology tended to prefer works that could be analyzed in depth independently of social context, particularly because their graduate education included little history, economics, science, religion, philosophy, or art, they recommended to textbook companies philosophically complex works that they could relate to other literature in the canon. In time it was to a large extent the textbook companies, aided by professors, who defined the "tradition" that Eliot saw overarching Western culture. And the textbooks could easily reproduce discrete texts already certified as valuable to students.

The isolation of the work from its context served academics well politically in the anti-Communist purges of the late forties and fifties, because the literary establishment had selected for aesthetic study a set of "masterpieces" whose political intentions (as Tate had convinced many) fell outside the range of literary study. According to two recent critics of the ideology of New Criticism, Bruce Franklin and Richard Ohmann, New Criticism blocked the entrance of proletarian ideas into the discipline in the thirties and then served anticommunism in the fifties (B. Franklin, "Teaching" 114). By putting literature above social process, New Criticism made explicit what Cartesian dualism had always asserted implicitly: the privileging of mind over matter, of thought over action, of art over society, of intellectual over laborer. The New Critics, like the Humanist defenders of literature before them, pitted literature against science, against business and industry, against vulgarity, and against politics (Ohmann, "Teaching" 152–53). In so doing they supported the principle of academic freedom, which allowed freedom of speech within discipline: they had defined the discipline in such a way as to exclude politics.

Within the academy, New Criticism built in the means to perpetuate itself. As universities opened up to students of all classes, New Criticism had enabled professors to teach ways of reading texts to students who did not possess broad cultural knowledge (Hartman 285). And whereas generally only older scholars had the experience to discuss and to write of literature in historical contexts, younger scholars, many of whom themselves lacked broad cultural knowledge—in part because of the discipline's demand for specialization within literature—could criticize individual works well in the classroom and in short articles. The university expectation that professors of literature would do research (of the sort that administrators could measure—articles and books) within limited periods of time encouraged scholars to select, in Cartesian fashion, parts of "the tradition" for examination, usually those works already approved by their colleagues for possessing enough philosophical and formal complexity to warrant professional attention. By legitimating as scholarly research the intense scrutiny of individual literary works in isolation, New Criticism allowed great productivity. The numbers of journals, regional conferences, and Modern Language Association sessions devoted to the analysis of individual canonical works increased in proportion to the demand on the untenured to demonstrate their analytical skills and acquire professional visibility. And those who avoided Marxist approaches offered little threat to the literary establishment. In imitation of the sciences' research model, New Criticism thus provided for specialization, objectivity, and quantifiable research, for which reason only a radical critique of the whole academic structure, and with it a radical critique of the dualist paradigm, could dislodge it. But that was to come.

A Room of One's Own, based on two papers Woolf read to the Arts Society at Newnham and the Odtaa at Girton in 1928 and published in 1929, outlined—in a tentative, conversational style—a critique of the literary canon that for later feminists and leftist critics turned canonical works into documents of social history. This critique represented in effect a "danger" to the discipline of literary study that moved Tate, over ten years later, to argue against historical and political interpretations of the literary work. In an imaginative account of her attempt as a woman to do literary research, Woolf challenged the authority of the canon by asking: "Why was one sex so prosperous and the other so poor? What effect has poverty on fiction? What conditions are necessary for the creation of works of art?" (25). Why was woman pervasive in poetry and absent from history? (45). Why did women not write poetry in the

Elizabethan age? (47). How could a woman have written without "a room of her own"? (54). Why did (a few) women choose to write novels? (68). If women wrote novels, and if novels conveyed social values, why did masculine values prevail? (76–77). Was the "man's sentence" appropriate for women's writing? (79). Why must society establish a hierarchy of literature?

> All this pitting of sex against sex, of quality against quality; all this claiming of superiority and imputing of inferiority, belong to the private-school stage of human existence where there are 'sides,' and it is necessary for one side to beat another side, and of the utmost importance to walk up to a platform and receive from the hands of the Headmaster himself a highly ornamental pot. (Woolf 110)

With these questions Woolf introduced an investigation into the constitution of the canon that became a critique of the culture's construction of reality. The habit of evaluating things according to their perceived position in a vertical hierarchy, an effect of the belief in the superiority of the spiritual over the material, organized the whole of society: socially, by giving the aristocracy power over the proletariat; philosophically, by giving intellectual knowledge prestige over technical skill; sexually, by giving men authority over women; literarily, by canonizing those works that addressed the themes and forms of the "tradition." By focusing on the "material" reasons for which society had canonized some texts and not others, Woolf implicitly questioned the intrinsic value of canonical works. If works were not intrinsically "canonical," then did the culture need to continue the practice of assessing a work's superiority or inferiority to others? In short, were not literary values relative?

The reification of utterance into text and then, with the culture's glorification of the author, into "work" had in the end eliminated from the culture's intellectual consideration the very discourse that had produced "the tradition." For the dualist vision did not encompass those utterances from which its intelligentsia selected "the best that is known and thought in the world." Yet by the time Woolf wrote *A Room of One's Own*, various other thinkers were challenging the basic assumption on which Eliot's literary tradition rested, that of the human mind's independence of matter. Darwin had shown that human consciousness originated in matter and that the human being had evolved from simpler organisms. Marx had argued that individual consciousness depended on the structure of society and that "geniuses" were not originators of ideas but were themselves produced by social movements, thus initiating a nondualist investigation into the nature of consciousness. Freud had contributed to the debunking of the Romantic concept of poetic genius by attributing art to human pathology: "a happy person never phantasies, only an unsatisfied one. The motive forces of phantasies are unsatisfied wishes, and every single phantasy is the fulfillment of a wish, a correction of unsatisfying reality" (9: 146). In opposition to critics influenced by Darwin, Marx, and Freud, the New Critics had striven to "save" literature by deprecating historical, biographical, sociological, and psychological approaches to the "verbal icon," in hopes of turning attention away from society and toward the work itself. Woolf, in the self-effacing style of her book's narrator, asked about society.

With her questions, Woolf contributed to a mode of cultural self-reflection that came to characterize twentieth-century philosophical, social, literary, and even scientific thought, to which the feminist movement eventually offered a thorough critique of the methodology and presuppositions of orthodox literary study as well as of various other disciplines. If one needed economic freedom to have intellectual freedom, then spirit was inseparable from matter. If one needed a classical education to obtain the "historical sense" required to enter into dialogue with other works of "the tradition" or even to appreciate those works, then spirit, to which those works spoke, was dependent upon social rank. Did spirit belong only to the economically comfortable? If male values rather than female values dominated the works canonized, did only men possess spirit? If not, then what social forces gave men the political power to determine the canon and to force their values on the reading public through "the tradition"? If spirit was inseparable from matter, then "literary texts," which had served in the dualist paradigm as the expression of the human spirit, were not intrinsically distinct from other texts, such as all the uncanonized women's novels.

Two years before Woolf published *A Room of One's Own*, Heisenberg had presented his Indeterminacy Principle, recognizing that the investigator of "reality" affected the object of observation by that very investigation, that what the investigator could know, at the level of subatomic particles, was affected by the instruments and methods of investigation. Heisenberg himself later elaborated its philosophical implications: that our knowledge of the world was related to our values, to what we looked for, to how we looked, and to what we were predisposed to find. The relativism born not only of physics but also of art, of the earlier Impressionists' recognition of the observer's inextricability from the object of observation, and of Darwinism, Marxism, and Freudianism, yielded a twentieth-century holism: the recognition that discourse, always relative to its culture, determines human reality and that therefore subject and object (self and world), which are constituted by discourse, are interdependent and inextricable.[3] And if the culture's discourse—its writings, its utterances, its economic exchanges, its role definitions, its social relationships, its alliances, its wars—determined what appeared to be an objective external reality, then many of the "truths" that society had taken for granted were historically grounded social fictions.

Because dualism had kept the disciplines of literary study and science ideologically distinct from each other for three hundred years, the early twentieth-century relativism in science was slow to change academic literary study. Most literature professors, long into the twentieth century, held Arnold's belief that the best thought and written should naturally constitute the subject matter for literary scholarship and teaching: the best literature, according to this assumption, naturally constituted the canon. And "the best" embodied values that supposedly were culturally "universal."

Like the canon of sacred texts, the canon of secular texts had developed in response to a desire to comment on them,[4] and by reorienting the discipline from scholarship to criticism, the New Critics altered the literary canon they had inherited from nineteenth-century literary scholars. The practice of literary interpretation had come out of dualism: from Biblical exegesis; from print literacy's reification of the utterance; from the secularization of the culture which yielded literature as a substitute for sacred texts for knowledge of the world; from the distinguishing of the literary "work" (as a product of its author) from the scientific, historical, or political text; and from the opposition of modern literary study to science in the university. By setting literary works above other texts, the culture established the necessity to comment upon them; and by making literature the subject matter of a discipline, that of literary study, higher education turned that commentary into research and teaching practices.

Commentary on texts became critical interpretation of texts when literature professors clarified both their discipline's difference from other disciplines, such as history, sociology, and linguistics, and their discipline's methodology: that clarification involved an explicit recognition of the subject/object relationship of the literary critic to the work, with a call to examine the work itself. In order to define and legitimate the discipline's academic territory, the New Critics revised the canon in such a way as to include primarily those works of sufficient complexity in and of themselves to justify intensive scrutiny. Focusing on written texts, they almost inevitably excluded imaginative verbal material by blacks and Native Americans, whose lack of a print-literacy tradition affected the subject matter of their song and verse; and they almost inevitably excluded that of women whose choice of subject matter placed them outside Eliot's "tradition." As Nina Baym argues, the apparent discrimination against nonwhite, nonmale writing was probably unintentional:

For example, suppose we required a dense texture of classical allusion in all works
that we called excellent. Then, the restriction of a formal classical education
to men would have the effect of restricting authorship of excellent literature to
men. Women would not have written excellent literature because social conditions
hindered them. The reason, though gender-connected, would not be gender per
se. (65)

According to Baym, the later identification of an American myth—the confrontation of the individual ("the pure American self divorced from specific
social circumstances") with the wilderness—served to elevate such writers as
James Fenimore Cooper and Herman Melville, to the neglect of women novelists concerned with home and children (71). The New Critics thus tended to
leave out of the canon texts of domestic, regional, or political concerns that
did not appear to transcend the material, many of which belonged to powerless groups in society who could not afford—or had no desire—to neglect
their immediate circumstances in their fiction, poetry, or song. Those in
power, the literary establishment (composed mainly of white, middle-to-
upper-class men), could indeed ignore politics, and could believe that their
"objective" approach to great literature implied no ideology.

In the twenties and thirties the major poetry anthologies tended to organize
poems according to poets (of whom the black poets James Weldon Johnson,
Paul Laurence Dunbar, Claude McKay, Jean Toomer, Langston Hughes, and
Countee Cullen were well represented, as were many women) or according to
such categories as American Indian Poetry, Negro Spirituals, and Backwoods
Ballads.[5] In *Understanding Poetry*, however, Brooks and Warren organized
the poems in such a way as to foreground "poetic" characteristics rather than
authors or ethnic categories, for reasons they explained in their "Letter to the
Teacher": "Though one may consider a poem as an instance of historical or
ethical documentation, the poem in itself, if literature is to be studied as literature, remains finally the object for study" (iv). Disregarding chronology, they
divided the poems into seven sections: Narrative Poems, Implied Narrative,
Objective Description, Metrics, Tone and Attitude, Imagery, and Theme, in
each of which they included poems from various centuries. Although they
stated that "it is not to be understood that the topics which determine the
arrangement are treated in isolation" (x) (that is, independently of historical
or biographical considerations), by collecting the poems according to poetic
characteristics, Brooks and Warren reinforced the opposition of poetry to
prose and, by implication, literary to nonliterary, and thereby contributed to
later critics' rather exclusive attention to literary works alone. And although
they reiterated that poetry was not "separate from ordinary life" (8), and that
content was inextricable from form, by disengaging the "message" from the

appreciation of the poem itself (10–14), they ignored the ideological content of literature, as well as their own ideology hidden in their treatment of it. *Understanding Poetry* contained (besides the anonymous poems) only 8 poems by women (by Amy Lowell, H.D., Emily Dickinson, Adelaide Anne Proctor, and Elizabeth Barrett Browning), out of some 240, and none by blacks, Native Americans, or "Spanish colonials."[6]

In their nineteenth-century search for the distinctly American, their late nineteenth-century demand for moral inspiration, and their early twentieth-century selection for universality, succeeding generations of editors had classified the verbal arts of Native Americans, Blacks, and women as less than "literary."[7] Little of the Native American oral poetry, black writing, or women's writing had the required characteristics. Literary scholars ignored the work of women for many reasons, as many recent feminist critics have pointed out. Much women's writing in America failed to be eligible for canonization because it fell outside the major genres of poetry, novel, and drama: women able to publish their work tended to publish short stories, books for children, travel literature, and educational treatises, whose usefulness and whose connection with daily life militated against their acceptance as American "literature" (Meese 38–39). Most nineteenth-century American women's novels, described as "sentimental" for their power to move their audience, did not enter the canon precisely because they did not meet the modernist aesthetic requirement of apparent disinterestedness: they belonged too little to "art" and too much to "life," in the dualist aesthetic/political distinction. Harriet Beecher Stowe's *Uncle Tom's Cabin* received credit by President Abraham Lincoln for starting the Civil War and yet, perhaps in part because of its political content, never won the designation of "literary" (Tompkins 81–104). Women's themes, in fiction, did not conform to the male critics' "American myth": that the American set out into the unknown to define *himself* in freedom from society, which was his adversary and which exerted "an unmitigatedly destructive pressure on individuality." Since women constituted the "society" which the American hero found repugnant, they were not inclined to write fiction supportive of that male fantasy and, consequently, were not likely to have their fiction recognized by the male critical establishment as being of universal appeal (Baym 71). Moreover, as Woolf argued in *A Room of One's Own*, few women's works entered the canon because few women had the privacy, the leisure, and the financial independence to devote themselves to intellectual life: "Intellectual freedom depends upon material things. Poetry depends upon intellectual freedom. And women have always been poor, not for two hundred years merely, but from the beginning of time" (112). Woolf herself was an exception.

So were the blacks poor, and mostly uneducated. Black writers in America generally did not share the literary establishment's values: black writers, those few with the literacy to write, seldom presented either the thematic or the formal patterns that critics sought as signs of aesthetic integrity; they could not afford to ignore the urgent material demands of their immediate circumstances to create a nonpolitical writing recognizable by modernist standards as art; they displayed little of the literary or philosophical sophistication that enabled writers to enter Eliot's "tradition"; they strove primarily to communicate to a wide audience; and they did not privilege the contemplative over the active life, because as a politically oppressed group they wanted social change.[8] The slave narratives, thousands of which appeared in America and England during the eighteenth and nineteenth centuries (Baker 31), were written to protest the injustices of slavery, and so were taken as political documents, of interest primarily to historians.

Native Americans were left out of the canon because Native American oral poetry was not considered "literature." In the eighteenth century the term "oral literature" would have been an oxymoron; and in the nineteenth century, after interest had developed in "Indian" literature, Native poems and stories appeared too "natural" to enter the canon, because of their ecosystemic perspective and their performative mode of presentation (Krupat 310–11). Despite efforts by such enthusiasts of Native song as Henry Rowe Schoolcraft in the mid–1850s and Frances Densmore and Natalie Curtis from 1901 through the mid-fifties to bring transliterations of Native song to the attention of the American literary establishment, Native American literature generally lost out to the internationalism of T. S. Eliot, Ezra Pound, and the New Critics.

To break into the canon, into the category of texts taught in English classes, many of the writings of blacks and Native Americans, as well as the writings of Chicanos, required a different mode of analysis—ideological rather than formalist—and a different purpose for literary study—cultural history rather than aesthetics. As Saussure said, "it is the viewpoint that creates the object" (8): the New Critical viewpoint uncovered few "literary works" by nonwhite, nonmale Americans.

Woolf, in calling attention to the dependence of intellectual freedom upon material comfort, unmasked the ideology of the dualist paradigm, an ideology that manifested itself not only in the capitalist exploitation of labor and the land, not only in the white's exploitation of other races, not only in the male exploitation of the female, but also in the intellectual's exploitation of the society that supported an intelligentsia to engage in the leisurely activity of thought. Although literary scholars tended to be generally liberal, opposed as they were to the utilitarianism of business and industry and attentive to human spirituality, in their dismissal of the political content of literature they rendered impotent in the academic world that literature written to bring about social awareness or social change. The New Critical discrimination of the "poetic" from the message allowed them to ignore not only the author's intention and the reader's reaction but also the author's own life, because art transcended life. In their view, neither did good poetry exhibit the particulars of the poet's life nor did good criticism evaluate poetry in relation to the poet's life.

The New Critics refused to consider not only left-wing political activities of writers but right-wing activities as well in their evaluation of poetic quality. In 1948, the Fellows of the Library of Congress in American letters, including Leonie Adams, Conrad Aiken, W. H. Auden, Louise Bogan, T. S. Eliot, Paul Green, Katharine Anne Porter, Karl Shapiro, Allen Tate, and Robert Penn Warren, awarded the Bollingen Prize "for the highest achievement in American poetry in 1948" to Ezra Pound for his *Pisan Cantos*. The jury decided that even though Pound was an expatriate American under indictment for treason, "to permit other considerations than that of poetic achievement would destroy the significance of the award and would in principle deny the validity of that objective perception of value on which any civilized society must rest" (quoted in Applebee 165).

The paradigm relegated to the realm of the material—and therefore the inferior—whatever appeared constrained by physical, social, or economic forces: that is, whatever lacked "freedom." The New Critics, whose material needs were not so pressing as to prevent their advocacy of a discourse proudly "useless" (with respect to economic power), appreciated least those works whose explicit ideological content required them to discuss politics, to leave the realm of the aesthetic for the inferior realm of the material. They appreciated most those works whose poetry apparently transcended the message, for those works engaged most demandingly the particular intellectual skills they had developed as specialists of literature. And they ignored those works whose unreflective "sentimentality" rendered foolish their rigorous methodology. Eliot's "tradition" gave them a basis for discriminating literature from nonliterature and for describing the relative values of works eligible for entry into the canon. Because Native Americans, blacks, and women did not address the literary issues of the "tradition," their writing was relatively uninteresting to readers who read texts independently of any nonliterary context; their works remained therefore uncanonized.

The 1968 MLA meeting, at which Louis Kampf, under arrest for passing out leaflets, was elected second vice-president, brought the issue of the discipline's ideology to the foreground.[9] And in the following years the radical left organized a systematic critique of the whole discipline for its orientation toward the individual, for its justification of literary study in terms of enrichment to individual lives rather than in terms of its relation to social structures (Bloland 72). Feminist, black, and leftist critics attacked New Criticism in particular for the implicit support its theories of literature gave to the political status quo. Since, as Woolf had said, the canon embodied primarily male values, then Tate's argument that literature offered "the only complete, and thus the most responsible, versions of our experience" made the canon into a social force to marginalize women and other groups whose values the canon did not represent. And Ransom's argument that the "object of a proper society is to instruct its members how to transform instinctive experience into aesthetic experience" validated art over political action as a means to cope with personal and social problems. The Brooks-and-Warren procedure for analyzing poetry, with its emphasis on "the poem as a poem," and the Wimsatt-and-Beardsley dissociation of the poem from its intention and its effect silenced poetry's political voice. Those who criticized the profession sought to disclose the inseparability of art from life, of literature from politics, of spirit from matter. They sought to show that the "mind of Europe," which for Eliot the literary canon expressed, depended "upon material things."

In seeing great literature as an ideal order of artworks comprising the mind of Europe, Eliot was engaging in a debate that had a long history. In 1820 Thomas Love Peacock had argued in "The Four Ages of Poetry" (with some humor) that "in whatever degree poetry is cultivated, it must necessarily be to the neglect of some branch of useful study: and it is a lamentable spectacle to see minds, capable of better things, running to seed in the specious indolence of these empty aimless mockeries of intellectual exertion" (18). To this Shelley had responded: "Poetry is indeed something divine. It is at once the centre and circumference of knowledge; it is that which comprehends all science, and that to which all science must be referred. It is at the same time the root and blossom of all other systems of thought" (70). Sixty years later Thomas Huxley stated, in a lecture titled "Science and Culture," that "for the purpose of attaining real culture, an exclusively scientific education is at least as effectual as an exclusively literary education" (141). Arnold replied in "Literature and Science":

> The more that the results of science are frankly accepted, the more that poetry and eloquence come to be received and studied as what in truth they really are,—the criticism of life by gifted men, alive and active with extraordinary power at an unusual number of points;—so much the more will the value of humane letters, and of art also, which is an utterance having a like kind of power with theirs, be felt and acknowledged, and their place in education be secured. (10: 68–69)

Arnold believed that the "humane letters" encompassed all human endeavors.

The debate continued. As recently as 1959, C. P. Snow bemoaned in his lecture "The Two Cultures" the lack of comprehension between scientists and literary intellectuals, "who [that is, the literary intellectuals] incidentally while no one was looking took to referring to themselves as 'intellectuals' as though there were no others" (4). Snow accused literary intellectuals of being "natural Luddites," who dismissed as "ignorant specialists" scientists who had not read Shakespeare but who were themselves impoverished because they pretended that the exploration of nature was of no interest either in its own value or in its consequences, as though "the scientific edifice of the physical world was not, in its intellectual depth, complexity and articulation, the most beautiful and wonderful collective work of the mind of man" (14). F. R. Leavis replied that there was only one culture and that "when human ends require to be pondered in relation to the pressing problems and opportunities with which our civilization faces us, one's thinking should not be blind to the insights given in cultural tradition," which was "a reservoir of alleged wisdom, an established habit, an unadventurousness in the face of life and change" (92–93), accessible through literature. Leavis went on to say, "There *is* an intrinsic human nature, with needs and latent potentialities the most brilliant scientist may very well be blank about, and the technologically-directed planner may ignore—with (it doesn't need arguing) disastrous consequences" (94). Literature provided knowledge of that "intrinsic human nature."

The dispute between humanists and scientists over the knowledge most worthwhile to the educated human being and most valuable to the culture as a whole arose with and is disappearing with the spirit/matter dualism. Bacon's seventeenth-century distinction between the kind of truth available to the humanities and that available to the sciences could last only as long as the culture's intellectuals believed in both a transcendent spirit, which encompassed the human soul or mind, and a mechanical universe which encompassed the body. As that dualism appears more and more to be an historical cultural construction, an illusion built into our language and our social practices, the competition between the humanities and the sciences over truth seems, as Woolf characterized the obsession with hierarchies, to "belong to the private-school stage of human existence where there are 'sides,' and it is necessary for one side to beat another side." In 1927 Heisenberg discovered limits to our possible understanding of nature, limits established by our own methods of exploration and by our values, thereby pointing the way toward an investigation into the social basis for scientific truths. In 1929 Woolf suggested that intellectual freedom depended on economic freedom, pointing the way toward an investigation into the social basis for cultural truths.

In 1940 Archibald MacLeish published in *The Nation* an article titled "The Irresponsibles," which attacked the whole academic establishment for fleeing responsibility for world events, particularly regarding Germany's threat to "civilization as men have known it for the last two thousand years." Mac-Leish predicted that future historians would ask:

> Why did we, scholars and writers in America in this time, we who had been warned of our danger not only by explicit threats but by explicit action, why did we not fight this danger while the weapons we used best—the weapons of ideas and words—could still be used against it? (618)

And he provided an answer:

> The scholar in letters has made himself as indifferent to values, as careless of significance, as bored with meanings as the chemist. He is a refugee from consequences, an exile from the responsibilities of moral choice. His words of praise are the laboratory words—objectivity, detachment, dispassion. His pride is to be scientific, neuter, skeptical, detached—superior to final judgment or absolute belief. (622)

Although many intellectuals praised MacLeish's essay for its "eloquence," not until the period of the Vietnam War did scholars seriously recognize that the idealized detachment of the academy from society and the division of knowledge into disciplines silenced humanists on matters of urgent concern to the culture. MacLeish had sided with neither humanist nor scientist; instead he had challenged the very premise of Anglo-American scholarship—"objectivity"—and had called into question the ethics of the dualist separation of intellectual work from politics. In so doing he anticipated the campaign that many Vietnam-generation intellectuals have begun to wage in various disciplines, the campaign for breaking down disciplinary boundaries, exposing the ideological foundations for our scholarly practices, and examining the social consequences of our teaching and research. It is the same campaign that Woolf inaugurated for the feminists, for some of whom scholarship has become a means of political activism.

In the emerging holism, humanist and scientist are ceasing to define themselves in opposition to each other; and in time scholars of all branches of learning will recognize the impossibility of "detachment." By the late 1970s, many literary critics had found Kuhn's notion of "paradigm," which he explained in his widely read *Structure of Scientific Revolutions*, useful for literary and cultural history; and some scientists and historians of science, having read Heisenberg's own philosophical meditations, had turned toward critical theory for intellectual tools to understand the directions that science was taking. Evelyn Fox Keller and Carolyn Merchant, bringing to science interpretive skills acquired from the humanities, have now amassed an audience of humanists, social scientists, and scientists for their exposure of the patriarchal bias of science since the seventeenth century. Fritjof Capra, Marilyn Ferguson, Alvin Toffler, and a host of others have ignored disciplinary boundaries completely to show the major paradigm change under way, a change that is manifesting itself not only in the academic disciplines but in our social relationships, our economic structure, our politics, our communications systems, our medical practices, and our ways of seeing. In the discipline of literary study, Richard Ohmann's *English in America* (1976), which revealed politics in our methods of teaching literature and English composition, has influenced a spate of books on the history of the profession, many of which appear motivated by the concerns MacLeish expressed, many of which advocate the humanist's resumption of responsibility for matters beyond his or her area of specialization.

In *The Turning Point* Capra commented upon a 1979 *Washington Post* story about the despair of prominent intellectuals over solutions to the nation's problems:

> As sources of their confusion or retreat the intellectuals cited "new circumstances" or "the course of events"—Vietnam, Watergate, and the persistence of slums, poverty, and crime. None of them, however, identified the real problem that underlies our crisis of ideas: the fact that most academics subscribe to narrow perceptions of reality which are inadequate for dealing with the major problems of our time. These problems, as we shall see in detail, are systemic problems, which means that they are closely interconnected and interdependent. They cannot be understood within the fragmented methodology characteristic of our academic disciplines and government agencies. Such an approach will never resolve any of our difficulties but will merely shift them around in the complex web of social and ecological relations. A resolution can be found only if the structure of the web itself is changed, and this will involve profound transformations of our social institutions, values, and ideas. As we examine the sources of our cultural crisis it will become apparent that most of our leading thinkers use outdated conceptual models and irrelevant variables. It will also become evident that a significant aspect of our conceptual impasse is that all of the prominent intellectuals interviewed by the *Washington Post* were men. (25–26)

Although, in the late twentieth century, more and more scholars are shunning specialization in favor of acquiring a broad knowledge of events and institutions and are challenging the academy's detachment from "the real world," they are less likely—so far—to be interviewed than are "experts," those obtaining renown through their disciplines. However, the academy is changing. Critics of the profession of literary study, feminists, and the new transdisciplinary thinkers of the "unified field" of "Theory," such un-disciplinary thinkers as Michel Foucault, Roland Barthes, and Jürgen Habermas, have all been working to expose the inadequacies of Cartesianism for late twentieth-century political and social practices. And in so doing, they may expose the inadequacy of the present specialist-oriented academic structure for the solution of global problems.

5

From Dualism to Holism

When we speak of the picture of nature in the exact science of our age, we do not mean a picture of nature so much as a *picture of our relationships with nature*. The old division of the world into objective processes in space and time and the mind in which these processes are mirrored—in other words, the Cartesian difference between *res cogitans* and *res extensa*—is no longer a suitable starting point for our understanding of modern science. Science, we find, is now focused on the network of relationships between man and nature, on the framework which makes us as living beings dependent parts of nature, and which we as human beings have simultaneously made the object of our thoughts and actions. Science no longer confronts nature as an objective observer, but sees itself as an actor in this interplay between man and nature. The scientific method of analyzing, explaining and classifying has become conscious of its limitations, which arise out of the fact that by its intervention science alters and refashions the object of investigation. In other words, method and object can no longer be separated.

—Werner Heisenberg, *The Physicist's Conception of Nature*

Criticism is literature or it is nothing.

—Leslie Fiedler, "Cross the Border—Close that Gap: Post-Modernism"

The question that now begins to gnaw at your mind is more anguished: outside Penthesilea does an outside exist? Or, no matter how far you go from the city, will you only pass from one limbo to another, never managing to leave it?

—Italo Calvino, *Invisible Cities*

L iterature, as a body of works supposedly distinguishable from other texts, texts that told empirical truths, depended for its definition in Western culture on dualism, as did the discipline of literary study. When dualism breaks down in the twentieth century—when philosophers and scientists acknowledge that neither language nor science can be value-free—literature loses its definition as uniquely value-laden discourse; and criticism, as the interpretation of the "literary work," dependent for its credibility upon the critic's "objectivity," appears another imaginative excursion, not intrinsically distinguishable from what was once called a "literary" text. If, as Heisenberg wrote, we can no longer separate *res cogitans* from *res extensa*, then, in Italo Calvino's words, "we cannot know which is inside and which is outside" (104). There is no longer any demarcation of mind from world: there is no objectively definable "external reality." Just as the scientist now focuses on "the network of relationships between man and nature," so does the new literary critic, who focuses on language and recognizes that the poem's meaning depends upon the reader and the reader's community and who is aware that if literature is not intrinsically distinct from other texts, then there is no literature—or there is only literature. So what becomes of the discipline of literary study?

Heisenberg's observation that the "old division of the world into objective processes in space and time and the mind in which these processes are mirrored—in other words, the Cartesian difference between *res cogitans* and *res extensa*—is no longer a suitable starting point for our understanding of modern science" (29) has become axiomatic for many scholars in the social sciences. About the time that Einstein published his paper on "The Special Theory of Relativity" (1905), Ferdinand de Saussure, lecturing at the University of Geneva between 1906 and 1911, developed a structuralist linguistics on the assumption that "far from being the object that antedates the viewpoint, it would seem that it is the viewpoint that creates the object; besides, nothing tells us in advance that one way of considering the fact in question takes precedence over the others or is in any way superior to them" (8). Edward Sapir and Benjamin Lee Whorf explored the implications of this linguistic relativity for the cultural perception of phenomena, and in so doing they demonstrated for linguistics the inseparability of form and content, language and "reality." For Sapir,

> Human beings do not live in the objective world alone, nor alone in the world of social activity as ordinarily understood, but are very much at the mercy of the particular language which has become the medium of expression for their society. It is quite an illusion to imagine that one adjusts to reality essentially without the use of language and that language is merely an incidental means of solving specific problems of communication or reflection. The fact of the matter is that the "real world" is to a large extent unconsciously built up on the language habits of the group. . . . We see and hear and otherwise experience very largely as we do because the language habits of our community predispose certain choices of interpretation. (Quoted in Whorf 134)

Whorf provided empirical evidence for linguistic relativity in his studies of the Hopi language, from which he deduced in 1939 that a culture's understanding of time and space depended on its language structure, and that, in Western civilization, "Newtonian space, time, and matter are no intuitions. They are recepts from culture and language. That is where Newton got them" (153).[1] By now most linguists and anthropologists generally accept a version of the Whorf-Sapir hypothesis, whereby a culture's language governs to some extent a culture's "reality," an assumption which goes by the name "prison-house of language" (originally Nietzsche's metaphor) in contemporary literary theory.

After Darwin had explained the origin of consciousness by reference to biological forces and Freud had explained psychic behavior by reference to the environment and to the unconscious, these linguists contributed to the twentieth-century deconstruction of self and world in explaining the culture's perception of phenomena by reference to its language, its discourse. The culture's discourse thus became the major focal point for cross-disciplinary critical theory in the latter half of the century. If a culture's understanding of space and time depends upon language, then the individual's understanding of events and relationships is socially constructed: both "reality" and self are, accordingly, constituted by the culture's discourse, which determines how the social community sees the world and how it imagines the self. Even the truths given by science, whether empirical or theoretical, acquired the appearance of relativity in light of Whorf's observation.

In 1953 Eugene Odum and Howard T. Odum published *Fundamentals of Ecology*, in which they demonstrated the interrelatedness of all biological phenomena and argued the futility of studying organisms, or parts of organisms, independently of their environment; in so doing the Odums established the new "integrative" discipline of ecology, a discipline concerned with systems rather than with isolated matter, which linked the natural sciences not only with each other but also with the social sciences.[2] In *Science* Eugene Odum wrote:

> If subjects were organized according to the literal derivation of their names, then ecology and economics would be companion disciplines since the words are derived from the same Greek root, with ecology translating as "the study of the house" and economics as "the management of the house." The disciplines remain poles apart on college campuses as well as in the minds of the general public as long as each restricts itself to only a part of the house, nature's and man's part, respectively. (Odum, "Emergence" 1292)

What scientific reductionism had separated, ecology attempted to reunite. In the structure of higher education and, accordingly, in the structure of our knowledge, the birth of ecology signaled the end of the philosophical opposition of the social world to the physical world.

The ideas of Darwin, Einstein, Saussure, Heisenberg, Sapir, Whorf, and the Odums have helped to bring about the "systems thinking" that is beginning to transform the presuppositions, methods, and professional practices of various disciplines. Historians acknowledge the relativity of historiography; anthropologists and sociologists recognize that the method of investigating social phenomena influences the data obtained; and many philosophers believe that language provides the limits and possibilities of thought. In dissolving the boundary between self and world, these thinkers have made meaning and definition relative to context, which is itself unbounded, for it includes the observer: meaning becomes contextual, and therefore unfixable.

In the holistic paradigm[3] a model of interaction and connectedness replaces that of opposition, a concept of network replaces that of vertical hierarchy, and a "top-down" approach to learning (that is, looking at the system first) replaces reductionism. When systems thinkers come to dominate the academy, eventually "integrative" fields may replace disciplinary departments. But that will require time; it will require that a new generation of intellectuals, born into a systems view of the world rather than into an atomistic or mechanistic view, who look to interrelationships and processes rather than to entities for their understanding of phenomena, discover a way whereby our academic structure may support a less discipline-bound search for understanding. When that happens, the humanities, or "holohumanities," as a *way of thinking* about events rather than as a body of works, will regain its relevance to society, to the new "global village" (in McLuhan's characterization of the postindustrial world), but in the process the discipline of literary study will be redefined.

While the holistic paradigm was developing in other disciplines in the first half of the century, in literary study professors were giving even such iconoclastic works of the avant-garde as Jarry's *Ubu Roi* the status of icons and devoting hundreds of pages to the supposedly objective interpretation of them. Until the late sixties the majority of literary scholars failed to recognize the implications for their own practices of the breakdown of the Cartesian paradigm which those works announced. New Criticism, which was founded on the critic's distance from and subservience to the literary work, dominated the profession.

A shift in paradigm takes place over a period of time with its participants usually not fully recognizing the implications of their own contributions to it. Monet and Picasso and later James Joyce and Gertrude Stein were repudiating, in one way or another, Cartesian dualism, in that each abandoned the realist aesthetic whereby art served as a window onto a scene or fictive event apparently external to the artwork. Over half a century later, in an equally iconoclastic manner, Roland Barthes declared the "death of the author," and a host of other flamboyant critics rejected the assumptions and practices of New Criticism with a verbal violence comparable to their artistic predecessors' rejection of realism. The wide variety of hyperbolic critical gestures of the past two decades (described by unsympathetic observers as "advanced cases of self-display" or "individualism gone to seed") issue from the search for a new order in a period in which the old order no longer holds and in an area of discourse—the humanities—in which the systems model is only beginning to install itself.

Now the defenders of traditional approaches to literature and the advocates of the new model confront each other with the passion of a theological dispute. To the defenders of literature as a privileged discourse, those negating a distinction between literary and other texts seem not to appreciate either the beauty of the poem or the originality of the poet; and to systems thinkers, those distinguishing between literary and other texts seem not to recognize the implications of relativity.

To the systems thinkers if there is no absolute difference between "poetic" and "ordinary" language, the difference between "literary" text and "scientific" text becomes problematic, as does the difference between literature and history; that difference had been posited on the basis of a distinguishability of human values from the world of facts, in the assumption that a value-free "ordinary language" could be used for investigation and description of that world of facts. Once language is shown to be always value-laden, whether in service of science, history, or fiction, literature loses its uniqueness as aesthetic discourse. Literature, according to Stanley Fish, is simply "language around which we have drawn a frame, a frame that indicates a decision to regard with a particular self-consciousness the resources language has always possessed" (108–9). What distinctions can be made must be made on the basis of the text's intention and effect upon the reader (what Wimsatt and Beardsley called the intentional and affective fallacies for the discussion of the literary work)—in other words, on the basis of the text's context. Insofar as the author's intention may be unknown, the reader judges the nature of the text, its purpose, and its truth value according to the position it occupies in the culture's discourse: the reader's interpretation of a text purporting to be literary will differ from that of a text purporting to be scientific.

The sciences, concerned in the dualist paradigm with the material world, accepted the systems model earlier than did the humanities, having undergone the theological upheaval at the time of Darwin's *Origin of Species*. The humanities, having combatted Darwinism with Arnoldian faith in the value of the best thought and written, did not experience the turmoil of paradigm shift until a hundred years later.

At stake in the late twentieth-century battle over the status of literature, as in the nineteenth-century battle over Darwinian evolution, is the concept of an autonomous self, the individual as origin of values and originator of ideas. The challenge to this belief, coming from France in the late 1960s and early 1970s in the form of "structuralism," implied a challenge to the concept of literature and therefore to the function of the discipline of literary study in society. Upon the assumption of a soul, or self, separable from body and world, had rested the discipline's belief in the possibility of an "author," a "genius," who externalized "original" ideas in literary "works," the interpretation of which yielded the spiritual—or aesthetic—"content," or "meaning," embedded in the work's form. Knowledge of this content was valuable to a society that believed in a spiritual reality (God) transcendent to the material universe which science explored and in a self transcendent to the material forces of the individual's environment; the academic discipline of literary study served society well by making literary knowledge available to individuals.

Structuralism, by focusing on language as a system of values into which the individual is born and within which the individual thinks, undermined both the confidence in the creator-author of the literary work and the belief in an external order of things that language could represent. For some structuralists, language organized the individual's reality. And their focus on the structure (the system) of our order of things, a structure apparent in anonymous fairy tales as well as in Henry James' short stories, yielded, as Terry Eagleton says, "a remorseless *demystification* of literature." According to Eagleton, "The Romantic prejudice that the poem, like a person, harboured a vital essence, a soul which it was discourteous to tamper with, was rudely unmasked as a bit of disguised theology, a superstitious fear of reasoned enquiry which made a fetish of literature and reinforced the authority of a 'naturally' sensitive critical elite" (107). Structuralism deemphasized both the uniqueness of a particular text and the uniqueness of a particular "self."

"Poststructuralism," developing as a critique of structuralism's unhistorical assumption of the universality of thought patterns, was even more radically antitheistic. For poststructuralists, meaning is never immediately present in a sign: in Jacques Derrida's "decentered universe," "the absence of the transcendental signified extends the domain and the interplay of signification *ad infinitum*" (249). All meaning is relative, since no God holds meaning in place. Consequently, the literary "work," once thought to close upon a signified, becomes a "text," according to Roland Barthes's description of the implications of relativity for literature, a text irreducibly plural in meanings, caught up in an endless network of other texts, and therefore without boundaries (*Image* 155–64). The "death of God" means the "death of the author," which Barthes announced in 1968, as well as the "death of the critic" (*Image* 147), for the loss of belief in God, as a spiritual governor over a material world and as a transcendent source of meaning, occasions a loss of belief in the literary work's fixed meaning, a loss of belief in the spiritual value that the literary work (as a secular substitute for the theological work) held for the individual, a loss of belief in the autonomous self capable of thinking independently of social forces, and a loss of belief in the objective interpreter. If the author is no longer a credible authority for or originator of the text's meaning, then the author is more accurately a "writer," who puts together in perhaps a new way ideas and opinions that are in the air at the time of the writing; the act of writing is not an externalizing of original ideas conceived prior to writing or outside language. The text lacks a single, intrinsic, recoverable meaning because every reader reads differently—according to sex, age, nationality, language, socioeconomic class, personal interests, fears, desires, and so forth: so the death of the Author is the birth of the reader, the reader being "the space on which all the quotations that make up a writing are inscribed" (Barthes, *Image* 148).

The distinction between author and critic begins to dissolve: both are writers, the latter not necessarily secondary to the former. What was the critic to do, the critic once dedicated to disclosing the literary work's hidden meaning? One possibility was to "deconstruct" texts, showing hidden ideologies and self-contradictions embedded in their language. Another was to expose ideologies hidden within the discipline's practices. A third was to play, or to entertain, like some of the "postmodernist" writers.

In the late sixties, when Leslie Fiedler wrote "Cross the Border—Close That Gap: Post-Modernism," some critics began to argue that much of the new American literature was no longer "modernist," that, in Fiedler's words, "the age of Proust, Mann, and Joyce is over" ("Cross the Border" 151). To Fiedler, postmodernist writers of the sixties were gleefully and irreverently entertaining the reader with few pretensions of creating metaphysically significant literature, believing that in a relativist world "literature" need not impart a serious message. What is "literature" anyway? Or, as in the title of Fiedler's later book, "What *was* literature?" Postmodernist writers ignore traditional genres, mixing poetry, prose, and dramatic dialogue, including lists and chirographic pictures in the text, acknowledging the reader's participation in the construction of meanings, demonstrating the very process of deciding what to write by trying out alternative narratives within the same piece of fiction, incorporating self-criticism within the text, and blissfully trespassing traditional boundaries between literature and pornography. Robert Coover writes in "The Magic Poker":

> The girls have gone. The caretaker's son bounds about the guest cabin, holding himself with one hand, smashing walls and busting windows with the other, grunting happily as he goes. He leaps up onto the kitchen counter, watches the two girls from the window, as they wind their way up to the main mansion, then squats joyfully over the blue teakettle, depositing . . . a love letter, so to speak.

○ ○ ○

> A love letter! Wait a minute, this is getting out of hand! What happened to that poker, I was doing much better with the poker, I had something going there, archetypal and even maybe beautiful, a blend of eros and wisdom, sex and sensibility, music and myth. But what am I going to do with shit in a rusty teakettle? No, no, there's nothing to be gained by burdening our fabrications with impieties. Enough that the skin of the world is littered with our contentious artifice, lepered with the stigmata of human aggression and despair, without suffering our songs to be flatted by savagery. Back to the poker. (29–30)

Instead of a "feigned history" (as Bacon had called fiction) Coover gives the reader a self-reflective narrative, one that reveals the writer's process of constructing an illusion. And, though hardly unique in transgressing conventional boundaries between literature and pornography, Coover calls attention within his narrative to social and literary conventions in remarking upon the scatological turn his story has begun to take. Although the narrator abandons the rusty teapot in favor of the magic poker, he indicates that he does so only as a matter of personal preference.

Coover's story has little of the traditional realism whereby the printed text presented a self-contained world in which the reader ostensibly had no part, nor has another sixties "novel," *Snow White*, into the middle of which Donald Barthelme inserts a questionnaire for the reader:

1. Do you like the story so far?   Yes (   ) No (   )
2. Does Snow White resemble the Snow White you remember?   Yes (   ) No (   )
3. Have you understood, in reading to this point, that Paul is the prince-figure?   Yes (   ) No (   )
4. That Jane is the wicked stepmother-figure?   Yes (   ) No (   )
5. In the further development of the story, would you like more emotion (   ) or less emotion (   )?
6. Is there too much *blague* in the narration? (   ) Not enough *blague*? (   )

7. Do you feel that creation of new modes of hysteria is a viable undertaking for the artist of today?   Yes ( ) No ( )

8. Would you like a war?   Yes ( ) No ( )

9. Has the work, for you, a metaphysical dimension?   Yes ( ) No ( )

10.   What is it (twenty-five words or less)?

_____

_____

_____

_____

_____

11. Are the seven men, in your view, adequately characterized as individuals?   Yes ( ) No ( )

12. Do you feel that the Authors Guild has been sufficiently vigorous in representing writers before the Congress in matters pertaining to copyright legislation?   Yes ( ) No ( )

13. Holding in mind all works of fiction since the War, in all languages, how would you rate the present work, on a scale of one to ten, so far? (Please circle your answer)

      1   2   3   4   5   6   7   8   9   10

14. Do you stand up when you read? ( ) Lie down? ( ) Sit? ( )

15. In your opinion, should human beings have more shoulders? ( ) Two sets of shoulders? ( ) Three? ( )

                                                    (82–83)

The questionnaire parodies the traditional reverence for the literary work as an aesthetic object belonging to a higher realm than that of politics (than that of Congress) and as a "verbal icon" replete with meaning independent of the author's intention and the text's effect upon the reader. By asking the reader whether his Snow White resembles the Snow White of the fairy tale, Barthelme dramatizes the contextuality of his fiction and, accordingly, the relativity of its meaning to the reader's literary experience. By asking the reader whether he or she recognizes the "prince-figure" and the "stepmother-figure," Barthelme turns his fiction into "metafiction," commentary on other fiction and on the conventions of reading and interpreting. By asking the reader whether the work has a "metaphysical dimension," Barthelme turns the desire for metaphysical significance into a joke. And by asking the reader to rank the work "according to all fiction since the War, in all languages," which the reader supposedly keeps in mind, Barthelme mocks the Western obsessions with vertical hierarchies, competition, and evaluation. Like Coover's narrator, Barthelme's narrator becomes a critic of his own narration: Is there proper character development? emotion? *blague*?

For Fiedler, such new postmodernist fiction (of which "The Magic Poker" and *Snow White* are simply examples, not necessarily better than other narratives)—"apocalyptic, anti-rational, blatantly romantic and sentimental"— demands a new kind of criticism:

> A renewed criticism certainly will no longer be formalist or intrinsic; it will be con-textual rather than textual, not primarily concerned with structure or diction or syntax, all of which assume that the work of art "really" exists on the page rather than in a reader's passionate apprehension and response. Not words-on-the-page but words-in-the-world or rather words-in-the-head, which is to say, at the private juncture of a thousand contexts, social, psychological, historical, biographical, geographical, in the consciousness of the lonely reader (delivered for an instant, but an instant only, from all of those contexts by the ekstasis of reading): this will be the proper concern of the critics to come. ("Cross the Border" 152)

In Fiedler's holistic view the literary work is not a container of fixed meaning, but rather a printed utterance whose origin and destination are of the world and whose meaning is therefore undecidable. The seriousness with which the New Critics announced the meanings of works appears in a decentered universe to be a foolish holdover of a paradigm gone by.

Interpretation has been the object of critique in America since the early 1960s, when Susan Sontag concluded "Against Interpretation" with this statement: "In place of a hermeneutics we need an erotics of art" (14). Ten years later Barthes published *Le Plaisir du texte* (*The Pleasure of the Text*), an erotics of reading, consisting of some forty-five fragments of writing about pleasurable textual encounters. In her essay Sontag pointed out that, since Plato, Western civilization's theory of art as representation has generated the "perennial, never consummated project of *interpretation*" and that, "conversely, it is the habit of approaching works of art in order to interpret them that sustains the fancy that there really is such a thing as the content of a work of art" (5). For her, it is this theory that has put art on the defensive, because it automatically produces the distinction between "content" and "form" whereby content is essential and form accessory. For all their arguments against paraphrase, and against the distinguishing of content from form, the New Critics unwittingly sustained that opposition in making interpretation of the literary work as an aesthetic object the primary function of literary criticism and indirectly privileged those works whose content was "serious." It is this reverence for the work as a container of an intrinsic and therefore transcendent meaning that Sontag, Barthes, and the various postmodernist writers have abandoned.

However, the word *interpretation* has undergone a change in connotation for postmodernist critics since Sontag published her article. For critics rejecting the notion that a text "contained" meaning, meaning that was supposedly intrinsic to the text, interpretation of the literary work as an aesthetic object in isolation from its context appeared increasingly futile, based as it was on the belief in a metaphysical reality transcendent to the political world. Postmodernist critics are employing the word now to mean not the disclosure of a text's presumed intrinsic meaning, but rather the process of constructing meaning in a text according to the text's context, which includes the interpreter. For Sontag, interpretation signified "proclaiming the meaning of . . .''; therefore, she was "against interpretation." For Fish, interpretation is the inescapable and endless process of making order, making meaning contextually; and interpretations depend primarily upon the interpretive communities that construct the expectations of the interpreters. In Fish's view, "interpretation is the only game in town" (355).

In the art world the twentieth-century rebellion against representation has made interpretation of the avant-garde artwork simultaneously necessary, because its meaning is not immediately intelligible; superfluous, because its meaning is obviously relative to other artworks (and texts and events) and to the interpreter; and suspect, because the interpretation is itself a creation. Malevich's "White on White" is uninteresting to anybody unfamiliar with the art world, just as Gertrude Stein's "Tender Buttons" is uninteresting to anybody unfamiliar with the literary world; both works comment upon the histories of their genres. The dualist assumption that such works contained meaning in and of themselves provided for the seriousness with which critics before Sontag treated "high modernism." Sontag, Barthes, and later Jonathan Culler, in his article "Beyond Interpretation" (*Pursuit* 3–17), in conjunction with Fiedler, Derrida, and the deconstructionists, are—in diverse ways— bringing literary criticism out of the dualist paradigm, which governed its practices through the middle of the twentieth century, into an accord with the avant-garde literary texts themselves, which since Jarry have explored the nonhierarchical world of relativism.

In *The Pleasure of the Text* Barthes describes reading not as a search for a transcendent meaning, but instead as an erotic pleasure that serves no ulterior purpose. "If I agree to judge a text for pleasure, I cannot go on to say: this one is good, that bad," writes Barthes. "No awards, no 'critique,' for this always implies a tactical aim, a social usage" (*Pleasure* 13). Interpretation is a continuous, pleasurable process: it has no end. That attitude on the part of the postmodernist who believes in no transcendent reality, no hidden content to the text awaiting discovery and interpretation, takes not only such texts as "The Magic Poker" and *Snow White* as objects of pleasure, but *Madame Bovary* as well, though it was written from within a different paradigm. And in reading for pleasure, in a nonhierarchical world, the postmodernist finds all the distinctions between genres and between "good" and "bad" texts to be of no absolute value.

Because many postmodernist writers challenge with their playfulness the reverence with which traditional critics usually treat literature, Ihab Hassan constructs a playful criticism, a criticism ostentatiously indistinguishable from "literature." Abandoning the scholarly formality of the traditional critical essay, Hassan discusses the manifestations of postmodernism in a style that employs various typefaces, lists, imaginary dialogues, quotations, fragmentary musings, and the chirographic mode of concrete poetry in his 1975 *Paracriticisms*. In the chapter "POSTmodernISM: A Paracritical Bibliography" he writes that "without a doubt, the crucial text" for postmodernism is

In a later equally unconventional text Hassan lists six characteristics of "the metaphysics of absence":

A. The Unmaking of Man.
B. The Unmaking of Literature.
C. The Unmaking of the Discrete Author, Reader and Text.
D. The Unmaking of the Book.
E. The Unmaking of Genres (including Criticism).
F. The Self-Unmaking of Semiotics.

("Re-Vision" 99–100)

Other critics have rejected the formalist approach in other manners. In 1979, in an exploration for the discipline's practices of the non-Cartesian reality in which mind and world are indistinguishable on any absolute basis, five Yale poststructuralists—Harold Bloom, Paul de Man, Geoffrey Hartman, J. Hillis Miller, and Jacques Derrida, who was associated at the time with Yale—published *Deconstruction and Criticism*, a group of essays, one by each, that exposed "the difficulty of locating meaning totally within one textual source" (Hartman viii). In his own contribution to the volume, "The Critic as Host," Miller says: "The poem, like all texts, is 'unreadable,' if by 'readable' one means a single, definitive interpretation" (226). After playfully exposing the myriad connotations of *parasite*, in response to the accusation that a deconstructionist reading of a work "is plainly and simply parasitical" on "the obvious or univocal reading" (217), he writes:

> It is as if the "prisonhouse of language" were like that universe finite but unbounded which some modern cosmologies posit. One may move everywhere freely within this enclosure without ever encountering a wall, and yet it is limited. It is a prison, a milieu without origin or edge. Such a place is therefore all frontier zone without either peaceful homeland, in one direction, land of hosts and domesticity, nor [sic], in the other direction, any alien land of hostile strangers, "beyond the line."
>
> The place we inhabit, wherever we are, is always this in-between zone, place of host and parasite, neither inside nor outside. It is a region of the *Unheimlich*, beyond any formalism, which reforms itself wherever we are, if we know where we are. This "place" is where we are, in whatever text, in the most inclusive sense of that word, we happen to be living. This may be made to appear, however, only by an extreme interpretation of that text, going as far as one can with the terms the work provides. To this form of interpretation, which is interpretation as such, one name given at the moment is "deconstruction." (231–32)

Playfulness does not reflect an absence of serious intention. Having brought into view by their relativism the dualist paradigm (invisible until it was superseded by the relativist, or the holistic), late twentieth-century critical thinkers are investigating a variety of strategies for understanding the implications of decenteredness and communicating a new model for making sense of the world. Their dramatization of the processes of narration and interpretation, whereby every individual understands words according to the connotations of which he or she is aware, indicates their acceptance of the responsibility of intellectuals to comprehend and communicate the contemporary paradigm. What keeps such writing from being meaningless to a community of scholars for whom no God holds meaning in place in the text is the interest intellectuals share in the exposure of ideology.

The "Yale critics" (as they were called then) have influenced a host of deconstructionists, much of whose writing, by its jargon, its lack of respect for the integrity of the work, and its seeming self-indulgence, has antagonized many: scholars who long for a New Critical past, in which the critic's task was to reveal the work's supposed intrinsic meaning, and scholars who desire a new cultural or political criticism that speaks in a language intelligible to intellectuals outside the discipline. Some of the latter group may have learned the implications of decenteredness for the institution of literature from Derrida and Miller but have responded to decenteredness differently from either the deconstructionists or Hassan, and have moved away from the concept of a discipline altogether; others, unmoved by the deconstructionists, have turned toward cultural history for other reasons. As Fiedler predicted, these academics are less concerned with the text's structure, diction, and syntax than with the text's context. And "context" may refer to the text's period of composition, its author's intention, other texts in its genre, the reader's historical situation, the reader's interests . . .

Having long recognized—since the publication of *A Room of One's Own*—that disciplinary knowledge implies an ideology and that only the exposure of that ideology can begin to remove the oppression women and minorities have suffered for centuries in a patriarchal culture unconscious of the social foundations of its "truths," feminists in particular have been instrumental in developing a new political criticism. Objecting to the style of presumed "disinterestedness" with which scholars in the discipline have analyzed texts, many feminist and black critics are blending criticism and autobiography to demonstrate the fallaciousness and perniciousness of the Wimsatt and Beardsley argument regarding the "affective fallacy." Ellen Cantarow begins her article titled "Why Teach Literature: An Account of How I Came to Ask That Question" with the sentence: "I was an undergraduate at Wellesley College from 1958 to 1962" (57). Katherine Ellis announces in "Arnold's Other Axiom": "I am an English major who is about to conclude twelve years of expensive education and begin to transmit what I have learned to succeeding generations of students" (160). Barbara Smith opens her essay "Toward a Black Feminist Criticism" with a discussion of the difficulty of writing about black lesbian writers as a black lesbian writer (168–70). For MacLeish the convention of "objectivity" signified social irresponsibility; for these feminists it disguises an ideology of oppression.

To varying degrees feminist scholars have been influenced by Woolf, who used fictive autobiography in *A Room of One's Own* to examine the institution of academic scholarship from the point of view of one excluded from it. In 1970 Lillian Robinson published "Who's Afraid of a Room of One's Own," where (in addition to mentioning her own imminent trial for political crimes, her own manner of dress, her own journey through the streets to a male friend's apartment, and her own memories of college) she analyzes Woolf's arguments in relation to the ongoing sexual revolution and thereby gives them currency. Robinson is but one of many who take up in the seventies the questions Woolf posed in 1929. Autobiography in such discussions of literature reveals both the reasons for which the writers may offer (unapologetically but nonetheless self-consciously) a nonstandard analysis of a text, event, or institution and the consequences upon the powerless of unacknowledged ideology. It constitutes a nondisciplinary, or rather antidisciplinary, discourse. White male scholars believing in the universal appeal of great literature and in the possibility of objectivity are more apt to find their own position in the profession irrelevant to their scholarship than are women, relatively new to the profession, who are aware of how men may find women's views eccentric. Representatives of powerless groups who have recently obtained a voice in the profession have been quick to note that texts have effects and that particular teaching methods institutionalize particular values; in order not to follow what some believe to be a male style of elaborating theory in detachment from practice (a dualist habit), these first-person critics, recognizing as did Woolf the inseparability of ideas from politics, make explicit the historical and biographical basis of their own ideas.

With the recognition of the relativity of values and meanings, feminists have contributed to the growing fascination with the discipline's history and with its current practices, as have blacks and other powerless minorities. In opposing the governing disciplinary assumptions and in questioning the philosophical and political foundations for respected disciplinary research methods, many of these scholars describe their work as cultural commentary: postmodernism for them brings the merging of literary criticism with history, sociology, anthropology, philosophy, political science, and biology.

One effect of Cartesianism was the propensity to partition "external reality" and then to treat its "parts" as intrinsic wholes, a practice derived from the assumption that reality was objectively definable to the impartial observer. Yet it was this very assumption that fashioned the "wholes," simply because the process of making order is a process of unifying experience into an intelligible pattern. The discipline of literary study not only has hypostatized certain texts as "literary works," discussable as integral units, constituting thereby the canon, but also has hypostatized certain periods by selecting a few apparently characteristic texts and then defining the periods by them: Neoclassicism—Racine's plays, Boileau's theory; Age of Reason—Pope's and Voltaire's writing; Romanticism—Goethe's *Faust*, the poetry and theory of Wordsworth, Shelley, Coleridge. This division of the continuum of all texts, into (1) the literary as opposed to the nonliterary and (2) the different "periods," definable by their salient characteristics, has governed the structure of the curriculum in literature departments and the areas of specialization for scholars. It reflects the larger cultural division of knowledge into disciplines.

Since Fiedler and Hassan introduced the term *postmodernism*, critics have taken for granted a significant difference between the modernism of Joyce's *Ulysses* and Eliot's *The Waste Land*, for example, and the postmodernism of Coover's "The Magic Poker" and Barthelme's *Snow White*. Yet each of these "modernist" works can be read postmodernistically to emphasize the means by which each displays a consciousness of language, an openness to the reader's construction, an absence of a center, and a playful irreverence toward literature itself, characteristics frequently cited as postmodernist. Perhaps the standard definition of modernism was actually a dualist construction, developed from the confrontation of the New Critics, who sought complex, self-referential works for their canon, with the art of Joyce and Eliot, an art which was itself a radical rejection of dualist presuppositions: in other words, the New Critics' dualist effort to distinguish the aesthetic from the nonaesthetic yielded their definition of the period and their understanding of its artworks as self-contained. The postmodernist critique, however, which issues from a cultural self-reflection whereby we human beings recognize our own rage for order, has led some critics into deconstructive rereadings of many texts of the past, in a search for the ways in which those texts once thought to be self-consistent units actually contain their own self-contradictions. And postmodernist criticism tends to eradicate traditional divisions. From the postmodernist viewpoint, Joyce and Eliot (the Eliot of *The Waste Land*) look postmodernist.

Sometimes, however, when a model of reality manifests itself simultaneously in both literature and criticism (if we assume that one may still distinguish between the genres), the criticism and theory of a given period may be peculiarly appropriate to the contemporaneous literature. Fiedler's enthusiasm for a new "con-textual" criticism, which in his opinion the postmodernist narratives demand, encourages scholars to privilege precisely those works (such as "The Magic Poker" and *Snow White*) that such criticism illuminates, thus establishing (in textbook anthologies and in MLA sessions) a postmodernist canon of texts that acknowledge their own instability of meaning. The process is circular; and because of the nature of this particular paradigm, which calls into question the dualist assumption of representation, much postmodernist criticism and fiction share characteristics of form as well as theme.

But there are other circles too. Although Fiedler came to his argument for a criticism of "words-in-the-world" rather than "words-on-the-page" from reading playful sixties novels that appeared to him to close "the gap between artist and audience" ("Cross the Border" 162), politically oriented critics, interested in the effect of the canon on students and the effect of the discipline on society, privilege other texts in their rewriting of the culture's history. Political criticism, also a criticism of "words-in-the-world," generates very different canons from that of Hassan and Fiedler and a very different critical discourse, for it has different purposes. Feminists, for example, have called attention to Kate Chopin's *The Awakening* and Charlotte Perkins Gilman's "The Yellow Wallpaper" not only for their "literary" value, long ignored by the male-dominated profession, but also for their depiction of women as victims of a social structure in need of reform. Scholars of black writing are rereading slave narratives in search of the "sub-textual dimensions of Afro-American discourse" (Baker 26); and scholars of Chicano writing are examining *corridos*, folk tales, historical narrations, and popular theater with the assumption that these forms express social, cultural, and historical interests more than personal or individual interests and that they show little of the psychological introspection that distinguishes much Western literature (Sommers 150). Arnold Krupat, a scholar of Native American literature, believes that the new movement toward cultural pluralism and away from monocultural purism, the movement toward racial and sexual equality, the ecology movement, and the antihumanism of contemporary theory may bring new attention to Native American literature (310–11). There is no escape from this circle, for the critic's values and interests make the hierarchy he or she perceives and/or wishes to institute.

What is evident in the late twentieth century is that the knowledge we have about the world is a response to the questions we have asked; and the questions we have asked come from our culturally specific construction of reality. Traditional literary history was a response to the expectations given the discipline by the dualist paradigm, and the new literary histories being made today, as revisions of the old, are in turn responses to the expectations generated by the holistic relativist paradigm. We cannot *not* make order, but with the awareness we now have that our order of things is a cultural construction, we can maintain (that is, attempt to maintain) a critical attitude toward the definitions we have given to phenomena, the divisions we have made among phenomena, and our ways of investigating the world.

Dewey wrote in 1909 that intellectual progress is accomplished in the abandonment, rather than in the solution, of many of the apparently insoluble questions given by the older paradigm: "We do not solve them: we get over them" (*Influence* 19). The transformation of spirit/matter dualism into holism, whereby for some thinkers literature becomes either nothing or everything, may ultimately give public voice to many writers on political matters.

Soviet writers obtaining asylum in the United States, such as Alexander Solzhenitsyn, have been disappointed that the novels and poetry that won them notoriety and danger in their own country have been attended to only as "literature" here, occasionally taught in comparative literature courses for their "art." Without censorship, novelists and poets in America suffer little danger from the government, but little attention either. In his 1967 "Letter to the Fourth National Congress of Soviet Writers" protesting censorship, Solzhenitsyn wrote:

> Literature cannot develop between the categories "permitted"—"not permitted"—"this you can and that you can't." Literature that is not the air of its contemporary society, that dares not pass on to society its pains and fears, that does not warn in time against threatening moral and social dangers, such literature does not deserve the name of literature; it is only a façade. Such literature loses the confidence of its own people, and its published works are used as waste paper instead of being read. (vi)

Yet it is censorship, with government persecution of writers who dare to challenge state authority, that often brings public notice to literature and makes writers into public heroes. The words of courageous writers matter politically—to the readers seeking knowledge in literature about "threatening moral and social dangers," and to the authors themselves, who expect their writing to be taken seriously. In a land where the government does not enjoy the people's confidence, poets can be leaders, for people look to them for alternate interpretations of the meaning of events. And people are hungry for such interpretations.

But in a land where elected government officials generally enjoy the voters' confidence, poets' interpretations are irrelevant to the daily lives of law-obeying citizens. In the United States publishers may print what they wish, and those relatively few authors who cannot find a publisher for their work may pay for private publication. The government ignores the words of the poets, despite its subsidy of their work through the National Endowment for the Arts. And the public has such a wide variety of printed matter from which to choose—encyclopedias, novels, poetry, self-help books, exposés of political scandals, autobiographies of movie stars, spiritual guidance, and pornography—that it hardly pays more attention to the words of a Nobel Prize winner in literature than to those of a psychic interviewed on television. Having accepted the academic definition of literature as imaginative writing (and, unconsciously perhaps, the Freudian definition of literature as "phantasy"—produced by somebody dissatisfied with "reality"), the public usually takes the Nobel laureate far less seriously on issues of social philosophy than it does the spokesperson for the President. Furthermore, the sheer quantity of books tends to equalize the value of the assorted texts for a public accustomed to free speech. So even the writer of fiction valued highly enough by scholars to be taught in literature courses enjoys academic attention only as an artist and public attention (if he or she acquires any) as an entertainer.

In exposing the consequences of separating the æsthetic from the political, and the consequences of teaching "literature" separately from "nonliterature," perhaps postmodernist thinkers will help return to the writer the public influence the discipline has denied him or her through the traditional practices of selecting a canon for universality, studying literature for its poetry, and isolating a work from its context. For by privileging the literary, as scholars of literature have done since Bacon's association of poesy with the divine, and by defining a canon in terms of formal complexity, in an increasingly technological society concerned with getting and spending, the discipline has alienated the public from the texts taught in the classroom. Even bookstores have contributed to removing "great works" from the public domain by categorizing books as "literature," "fiction," and "nonfiction" (in addition to "poetry," "drama," "religious," "animals," "women," "cooking," "self-help," and the like), with the effect of encouraging all those people who did not enjoy their literature classes in school to refrain from buying books classified as "literature." Now postmodernist professors, making little distinction in their courses between literary works and other texts, analyzing them all *con*textually as expressions of the culture's model of reality in a given period, as particularly brilliant interpretations of events, or as widely appreciated writing, have begun to make "literature" part of the "air of its contemporary society." In time, students of these courses may be less likely to identify the literary as that kind of text which one is obliged to read differently from other kinds and may therefore be more likely to enjoy reading.

Writers in the systems paradigm may benefit from their integration into the culture's social-political-intellectual life by way of being heeded by politicians, businessmen, and scientists. If they acquire the stature of intellectuals in a model of reality that no longer separates the intellectual life from the political, in the information age succeeding the industrial age, they will be appreciated as interpreters of events. And writers wishing to influence a public politically, bringing to view "social and moral dangers," do need an audience that expects to learn something important from their books. Such a hybrid as Robert Pirsig's *Zen and the Art of Motorcycle Maintenance*, called "creative nonfiction," appeals to an increasingly well-educated public.[4]

So does "the New Journalism," which literature professors have largely ignored, despite Tom Wolfe's declaration in 1973 that in the sixties such writers as Gay Talese, Hunter Thompson, Jimmy Breslin, and himself "never guessed for a minute that the work they would do over the next ten years, as journalists, would wipe out the novel as literature's main event" (9). Truman Capote's *In Cold Blood* (1965), Wolfe's *The Kandy-Kolored Tangerine-Flake Streamline Baby* (1965), Thompson's *Hell's Angels* (1966), George Plimpton's *Paper Lion* (1966), and Talese's *The Kingdom and the Power*

(1969), which used literary techniques to describe a murder, a hot-rod show, a motorcycle gang, the Detroit Lions football team, and the *New York Times* respectively, heralded the popularity of a new genre of writing that fell outside established disciplinary boundaries. It seemed neither fiction nor fact, neither literature nor journalism. Rocognizing in the American public a hunger for "realism," the New Journalists have taken for themselves the terrain of the traditional novel—society, manners, and morals—which many contemporary American novelists, devoted to fabulation and metafiction, appear to have abandoned; the New Journalists have become entertaining interpreters of our behavior. But because their writing is about actual events and practices, it is classified as "nonfiction," outside the scope of most scholars and teachers of twentieth-century American literature.

Perhaps the impotence of "literary" writers in our culture to effect social change is a consequence not solely of democracy, or freedom of speech, or the abundance of texts available for public consumption, but of capitalism itself, which makes the intellectual life secondary to the business of earning money. As an economic effect of the West's spirit/matter dualism, capitalism provided for the exploitation of land, of human beings, and of texts, all of which appeared to be "matter" to the extent that they could be exchanged for capital. By the twentieth century, in its profitable alliance with science in the Cartesian paradigm, capitalism had implanted in the minds of the populace the beliefs that science and technology could solve all social problems; that science was more consequential than the arts because it was concerned with facts rather than with subjective values; that specialists, particularly scientists, knew more than nonspecialists; and that wealth and political power determined the country's welfare, rather than literature, which was suitable mainly for leisure time.[5] This attitude constituted the Philistinism that Arnold and the New Critics thought literary study could decrease. The critique of the dualist paradigm set in motion by late nineteenth-century artists and early twentieth-century physicists, linguists, and philosophers, and explored more fully by many contemporary interdisciplinary and nondisciplinary theorists, has become in the writings of some thinkers, such as Foucault, a critique of capitalism, and a far more effective critique than the one offered by traditional literary scholars, whose definition of literature depended upon dualism.

The shift in paradigm from dualism to the systems model suggests a shift from nationalistic and imperialistic capitalism to other economic systems more appropriate to a global interdependency. In the recognition that our technology has led us not only to computer literacy and instant telecommunication, the benefits of which are incalculable, but also to worldwide pollution and nuclear weaponry, the public may turn to its intellectuals, its writers, its generalists, for help in interpreting the events of our age and for help in reassessing our values. Perhaps the fear of nuclear holocaust will make the public eager for interpretations of events different from those of its technologists and its politicians.

What happens to the canon, Eliot's "tradition," with the proliferation of texts by such varied writers as Coover, Barthelme, Pirsig, and Solzhenitsyn, all of whom professors of literature are teaching in the classroom? What becomes of the discipline's subject matter? The "canon revision" that has occupied the attention of scholars influenced by the feminist and black critique of the profession's ideology deserves another name, for "canon revision" implies the granting of canonical status to previously uncanonized, perhaps unread, texts. Calling into question the traditional standards for canonization and opposing outright the assumption that one may find universal criteria for evaluating literary works, many of these critics believe the day of the canon as the subject matter of the discipline to be over. Because the ranking of texts in relation to each other depended upon spirit/matter dualism, as a justification for vertical hierarchy, and upon belief in "the aesthetic," the canon loses its authority as the best thought and written when its egalitarian interpreters conceive of reality more on the model of a network than on that of a Great Chain of Being and conceive of "literature" as a historically based construction. Moreover, because the existence of the canon depended upon a secondary kind of writing devoted to the interpretation of canonical works, to the disclosure of the valuable meaning contained therein, the canon loses its authority as the keeper of universal values when its interpreters demonstrate meaning to be not intrinsic but relative to the reader, value to be culture-specific, and criteria of "universality" to be determined by those in power.

Now we recognize that the publishing industry, rather than a supposed universal appeal of the canonized works, has helped to maintain the canon, determining primarily on the basis of the market the availability of texts to the public and consequently, to a great extent, the courses' syllabi. With the advent of copy machines, however, faculty are departing freely from publisher-enforced curricula by selecting and making immediately available to students new or previously ignored texts (a practice that raises legal questions regarding the copyright). Thus, as literary scholars recognize the implications for the canon of the decentered universe, access to instant copying accelerates the introduction of uncanonized texts into the curriculum. Not only Heisenberg and Derrida but also Xerox and IBM are bringing the systems paradigm to the academy.

Postmodernist critics, skeptical of the formation of a new canon, are discussing the fiction of Coover, Barthelme, Pirsig, and Solzhenitsyn in ways quite different from those of Bradley, Eliot, and the New Critics, and are "interpreting" those texts in ways that Sontag and Barthes would approve. Shifting attention from the canon to the discourse that constitutes the canon, in keeping with the relativist paradigm's shift from a presumed external reality as the object of empirical attention to our methods of investigation and our culture's order of things, postmodernists study texts (historical documents, political tracts, science fiction, ethnic song, and autobiography, as well as poetry, fiction, and drama) as indexes to cultural preoccupations, as expressions of particular (not necessarily universal) human experiences, and as generally acclaimed interpretations of phenomena. These scholars are looking at the reasons for which some texts have been selected for canonization and others excluded, some texts selected for anthologies and others excluded, and some texts kept in print and others allowed to go out of print; a few are teaching the history of the discipline, as Gerald Graff advocates, giving insight into the culture's division of knowledge by exploring the ideological conflicts that shaped the discipline (258). Examining a variety of writings with both the skills of "close reading" that the New Critics bequeathed to the profession and the relativism that Saussure, Woolf, and Derrida contributed, postmodernist teachers are returning "literature" to its pre-Romantic meaning of a category of written texts, before literature meant imaginative writing.

But how do we discover what we may want to read and teach? Finally, the relinquishing of the traditional canon as the discipline's primary subject matter may, to some extent, bring back a traditional function of criticism: public criticism of texts. The *freedom* to select from a multitude of texts is also the necessity *to select*, and selection requires knowledge. After New Criticism encouraged a generation of scholars to refrain, in quest of objectivity, from inserting obviously their opinions into their descriptions of literary works, the new relativism may inspire scholars to comment on a variety of texts with regard to their appeal to particular audiences; their contextual significance; their style, structure, and message; their value as cultural information; their political and moral implications; and their social effect. By challenging the traditional figure-ground relationship of text and context, postmodernist thinkers have brought into view many questions that were formerly obscured by the generally agreed-upon assumption that canonical works constituted the discipline's subject matter. And after becoming aware of the ideology implicit in the traditional New Critical methodology, some postmodernist thinkers, among whom number many feminists, have defined their task as commentary on culture and have expanded the audience of their writing far beyond the profession.

Postmodernist critics take seriously such insights as Sapir's—"that the 'real world' is to a large extent unconsciously built upon the language habits of the group"—in looking to the political implications of the culture's accumulated "knowledge." Just as feminists have recognized that the linguistic use of the pronouns "he" and "him" to indicate an unspecified individual and the word "man" to indicate humanity in general implies to the world's English-speaking population that men more visibly than women compose the human world, postmodernists are alert to the ways in which what the culture defines as "knowledge" or "truth" affects different individuals. *How* the culture articulates its understanding of events—linguistically, symbolically—determines how individuals position themselves and conceive of themselves in relation to what the culture has deemed important. Since, for these thinkers, there is no escape from ideology, the academic world can operate fairly and valuably to the society that supports it by examining the politics of discourse. (Paradoxically, the Christian fundamentalists attempting to throw out of the public schools third-grade textbooks as well as *The Wizard of Oz* for implanting ideas of "secular humanism" in the minds of children share with the postmodernists the recognition that all education imparts ideology.)

The holistic paradigm will probably be characterized by a *pluralism* of approach and interpretation: if there is no external reality subject to partition and definition, then different viewpoints generate different understandings of events, benefiting the culture in different ways. And this applies to literary history as well as to ecology. When we focus on Barthelme and Barthes, we may well conclude that postmodernism is marked by playfulness of writing and of reading; but when we focus on Pirsig, in apparent contrast, we may conclude the opposite, that postmodernism is characterized by a mixture of philosophy and fiction within the same text. With respect to criticism, we find that a structuralist approach to a genre produces a kind of knowledge different from that produced by a psychoanalytic approach to the particular texts of that same genre, which is in turn different from that produced by a feminist approach. And in the classroom, we find that juxtaposing literary texts with works of painting produces a kind of knowledge different from that produced by the juxtaposition of literary texts with political documents or economic statistics. Different teachers, with different notions of how students may best be affected by what they read, will establish different course syllabi, just as different critics—academic scholars and cultural commentators—with different notions of how the public may best be affected by what they read, will call attention to different texts. Although many professors in the discipline may describe such pluralism as chaos, it may ultimately lead to a greater appreciation of the power of words, and that appreciation was once the major concern of humanistic study. So when we focus on our own culture's process of making order, in our "reconnection" of *res cogitans* and *res extensa*, we may acknowledge that since the understanding we have of our world depends upon our particular processes of investigation, we need a multitude of interpretations.

In the relativism of the holistic model, we intellectuals must accept the relativism of our own arguments. And we must resist the Cartesian inclination to assume that the order we make of events, the interpretation we give, is "correct"—or "incorrect." Because the histories we write are histories we make according to the particular texts we select on which to focus our attention, texts which then take on the appearance of centrality to a mode of thinking, our own interpretations of texts are themselves subject to future interpretation by investigators of our order of things. So we may save ourselves from insoluble conflicts with each other if we admit our relativism. ("Correctness" as a concept belongs more to a dualism in which the belief in an objectively definable external reality makes statements provable than it does to a relativism; the parallel concept for the relativist or holistic paradigm should perhaps be "convincing.") However, our relativism does not mean a release from the consequences of our arguments; to the contrary, the end of the spirit/matter dualism, which separated the intellectual world from the political, means that we must *all* accept responsibility for the political implications of our words. In the holistic paradigm, writers, no longer designated "literary," "academic," "scientific," or "political," may all be considered interpreters of events, differing from each other according to viewpoint, no one of whom will necessarily be irrelevant to a complex global community.

In Calvino's *Invisible Cities* Marco Polo tells Kublai Kahn of all the cities he has visited, each distinct from the other and yet all, somehow, reminiscent to Marco Polo of the Venice he left behind. There is the city of Tamara, which "makes you repeat her discourse, and while you believe you are visiting Tamara you are only recording the names with which she defines herself and all her parts" (14). There is the city of Eutropia, where as time passes "the inhabitants repeat the same scenes, with the actors changed; they repeat the same speeches with variously combined accents; they open alternate mouths in identical yawns" (64–65). There is Beersheba, where the citizens believe that "suspended in the heavens, there exists another Beersheba, where the city's most elevated virtues and sentiments are poised, and that if the terrestrial Beersheba will take the celestial one as its model the two cities will become one," and that "another Beersheba exists underground, the receptacle of everything base and unworthy that happens to them" (111). Kublai Khan listens eagerly to Marco Polo, wishing to possess his own empire by knowing it, for "only in Marco Polo's accounts was Kublai Khan able to discern, through the walls and towers destined to crumble, the tracery of a pattern so subtle it could escape the termites' gnawing" (6). Yet after many visits from Marco Polo, Kublai Khan despairs: "By disembodying his conquests to reduce them to the essential, Kublai had arrived at the extreme operation: the definitive conquest, of which the empire's multiform treasures were only illusory envelopes. It was reduced to a square of planed wood: nothingness" (123). *Invisible Cities* offers a parable for the shift in paradigm from dualism to holism, from the focus on and desire for an object (with meaning supposedly intrinsic) to a focus on relationships and on discourse. And discourse is endless, forever escaping definitions and summaries.

6

Holistic Practices

It is forgotten that not our world, but we human beings are the cause of our problems, and that only by redesigning our thinking and acting, not the world around us, can we solve them.

—Ervin Laszlo, *The Inner Limits of Mankind*

The thesis of this book, *Reconnection: Dualism to Holism in Literary Study*, is that literary study as a discipline obtained its definition, purposes, methods, and philosophical justification from the Cartesian dualist paradigm and that the ending of that paradigm means the ending of the discipline—or its transformation.

In that dualist model of reality, in which mind was apparently separate from world, the purpose of the academy was the disclosure of Truth. Distinguishing intellectual endeavors from politics and business, professors of both science and literature in the late nineteenth century argued for "academic freedom" on the grounds that an intelligentsia, consisting of specialists in diverse fields of knowledge, allowed to pursue truth without interference from political groups, benefited society. And society accepted the notion of the university as an "ivory tower," even as land-grant institutions were establishing technological and professional schools to serve the public directly. But now, in the late twentieth century, the philosophical acknowledgment that the culture's intellectual life is inseparable from its political life has become a public issue, inspiring debate on the limits to academic freedom imposed by the government through federal grants and affirmative action laws and by industry through the merging of private corporations and public universities in scientific research. The crisis within the discipline of literary study therefore reflects the crisis in our model for understanding the world and in the academic structure where we set directions for further understanding.

The entire culture is in a period of massive, fundamental change, and it needs intelligent cross-disciplinary thinkers to ponder the effects of our technology and of our laws. I believe that a *restructured*, "holistic" discipline of humanistic study may help develop these thinkers, and I call that new discipline "holohumanities" to indicate its orientation toward the *whole* of society. The word "humanities" alone is insufficient, for it still suggests a subject matter (primarily languages, literature, philosophy, and history), rather than an approach, and an opposition to the physical and natural sciences, to the social sciences, and to politics and business. The function of holohumanities is connection, or "reconnection."

In 1940, warning the discipline of the danger he saw in "the totalitarian society . . . coming in the next few years," the New Critic Allen Tate argued (with the Nazis in mind) that the only way to save literature from political censorship was to consider it as a "form of knowledge" independent of politics (4, 8). In his article "The Present Function of Criticism," Tate said that consideration of the literary work as a historical, sociological, or political document not only compromised its aesthetic purity and the universality of its reference but also invited suppression by those who found its political implications dangerous to society; a solution to the dilemma was to disengage the work as an aesthetic object from its social context, thereby saving both literature from censorship and literary critics from political suspicion. Tate was adapting for the subject matter of his discipline the principle of academic freedom that President Eliot of Harvard had invoked to protect science from sectarian groups hostile to Darwinian biology: according to that principle academics refrained from commenting upon political matters in return for protection from political groups.

The separation of the academy from politics is being undermined now by both private citizens and academics. Sixty years after the Scopes decision was overturned and thirty years after McCarthyism seemed to have disappeared, the problem of right-wing efforts to control education—from elementary school through college—has arisen again. Maintaining that their right to their own religion releases them from any obligation to study evolution, various Christian fundamentalist groups have pressured state legislatures, independent school districts, and textbook companies to integrate "scientific creationism" into the curriculum as an alternative theory of human development and to remove from public school libraries textbooks imparting what they perceive as "secular humanism." If they have not done so already, they may soon demand the dismissal of teachers who do not share their views.

But it is not only the political right that is challenging educators in the courts to respect what they regard as rights guaranteed by the Constitution; academics on the political left are suing universities for sex and race discrimination in hiring and promotion processes. The involvement of civil juries in assessing promotion dossiers (see *Chronicle of Higher Education*, July 23,

1986, 19–20) opens the way for the public to determine the constituency and hence the political orientation of academic departments. Paradoxically, the "leftist" proposition that discourse carries ideology—that, as Virginia Woolf said, "intellectual freedom depends upon material things"—sanctions both the Christian fundamentalists' and the feminists' attack on academic freedom as traditionally conceived. Yet most scholars, including those who recognize a social basis for truth and thus a relativity of truth, oppose vigorously any political restriction of research, publication, or teaching, arguing that the *pursuit* of truth—or "understanding"—requires an intellectual freedom to explore the world and to publish and teach the results of thoughtful inquiry without constraint by government or sectarian pressure groups.

Originally, academic freedom in America required both specialization and the dualist tenet that Truth was distinct from "the partisan view of one or another of the political parties" (in the words of President Harper of the University of Chicago). As Harper defined academic freedom in 1900, "A professor abuses his privilege of expression when . . . he undertakes to speak authoritatively on subjects which have no relationship to the department in which he was appointed to give instruction" or when "engaged within a narrow field of investigation, he undertakes to instruct his colleagues or the public concerning matters in the world at large in connection with which he has had little or no experience" (quoted in Dewey, "Academic Freedom" 8–9). Since the Vietnam War scholars have increasingly called into question both the restriction of academic freedom to area of specialization and the practice itself of narrow specialization in the humanities. Who may address the public "concerning matters in the world at large," if not the humanist? Who is responsible for making connections between ideas and political events? On the other hand, how do scholars maintain free inquiry in a society that acknowledges in its legal system an interdependence of academics and politics? What is the humanists' responsibility to society?

As our culture undergoes the paradigm shift from dualism to holism we must reexamine the fundamental premises on which our concept of the university has rested; we must reexamine our notions of the purposes of higher education in this country, the relationship of the academy to society, and our rationale for academic freedom and tenure. Since my concern here is the discipline of literary study, I wish to suggest changes for its disciplinary practices consistent with the philosophical assumptions of our time, so that the new discipline of holohumanities may be valuable to the whole society of the twenty-first century, the society which supports the academy.

Before attending to the question of how to restructure our profession, however, we must understand more fully the implications of our present practices.

Specialization in the dualist paradigm has meant a focusing on a particular body of material—an area of that presumed external reality available for investigation. In the current research model for literary study we specialize in graduate school in particular areas of the canon—for example, Renaissance English poetry, seventeenth-century French drama, the novel as a genre—under the presuppositions that the subject matter for the discipline is literature and that the function of scholars and teachers is to interpret literary works for students and for ourselves. Once we have obtained positions in departments we generally teach some freshman or sophomore courses in composition, language study, or literature, as well as some upper-division or graduate courses in our areas of expertise. Having studied little economics or science in graduate school, we are more comfortable considering literature apart from developments in science or economic history than we are exploring relationships among a variety of texts; so in undergraduate courses we use textbook anthologies which designate for us the canonical works worthy of students' attention, and in graduate courses we imitate those anthologies when we select primarily "literary works" to include in our syllabi.

We specialize in our research not only because we know basically only literature, and mainly only that literature within the areas in which we took our preliminary doctoral examinations (for we have learned not to venture into areas in which we are not expert), but also because we are judged by our superiors in the profession and in our own institutions according to the disciplinary research we do. Older colleagues who are specialists themselves are unlikely to accept as scholarly those publications that range beyond an author's field of expertise or that depart from standard methods of disciplinary research. Moreover, since the opposition of the academic to the practical world has manifested itself within the discipline as an opposition of scholarly or critical writing to journalism, with journalism deprecated as less demanding and therefore less valuable than scholarship or criticism, we are discouraged from ranging outside our areas of expertise to write to a wider audience.[1]

The pressure to specialize in a field of knowledge also comes with assistant professors' need to demonstrate their talent within six years of being hired by an institution. Having just completed dissertations on specialized topics, assistant professors usually do not know enough to do more than to investigate in depth a narrowly defined area, and so they continue the practice instilled in them by graduate schools, in the hope of having their articles or books accepted for publication before the sixth-year tenure review. To supplement their published work and to acquire "visibility" (also expected of them for promotion), assistant professors give twenty-minute papers on narrowly defined topics at regional conferences, most of them organized as miniature

MLA meetings, to audiences usually composed of other professors there for the same reason whose expenses are subsidized by their home institutions in the interests of promoting research. Because promotion review committees frequently demand outside letters of evaluation by scholars in the candidate's field of expertise, those candidates who have participated actively in the profession by attending conferences and making "contacts" are more likely to have outside supporters than are those who have worked quietly alone. And those candidates who have specialized are more likely to find specialists in their own areas who are familiar with their work and from whom they may request letters of evaluation than are those few who have not. Visibility means success to many scholars, in part because it is the indication of success to their evaluating department heads, promotion committees, and deans.

A multitude of journals, too many in any one "field" for a scholar to read regularly, publish these scholarly articles, articles on which the journals depend for their own survival. The journals serve several functions: they not only disseminate scholarly research but also call attention to their home departments, thereby attracting graduate students and increasing the reputations of the home institutions and of the faculty there; they benefit the members of their editorial boards, who participate visibly in the discipline's research enterprise by selecting and publishing the work of other scholars; and they publicize scholarly books through reviews and advertisements. In a survey conducted by *The Chronicle of Higher Education* (August 6, 1986), 62 percent of those responding in the discipline of "literature" assented to the statement "It is virtually impossible to keep up even minimally with the literature *in my field*" (21; emphasis mine). Of course: by defining a field as a body of knowledge, as an area of an external reality capable of being known, we academics have set before ourselves an impossible task—that of obtaining all the information available about that field—and with the profusion of information, with the proliferation of articles by academics, we shall never "keep up."

This research model, which mirrors that of the sciences in its structure of information exchange, defines a faculty member's value to the profession primarily by research productivity—that is, by rate and quantity of publication. And although it is obviously a reductionist model, encouraging specialization and orientation toward a product (the article or book), leaders of the profession find few alternatives in a decade in which the burgeoning of discrimination complaints necessitates the comparison of faculty members on ostensibly objective criteria. *The Chronicle of Higher Education* (August 13, 1986) reports that an official of a college being sued for discrimination, who was asked to turn over the files not only of the plaintiff but also of the other candidates for promotion, declared, "For the people who came up for tenure, our plan is to take off every identifying mark, but still give some idea of the *quantity* of publication" (20; emphasis mine). That college and others whose promotion files have been subpoenaed by the courts have defended their right to keep those papers confidential on the basis of academic freedom, which by presupposing a separation of the culture's intellectual life from its political life grants scholars authority to be the sole judges of each other's work. Yet the very suits that now threaten academic freedom issue from the discovery of discrimination against various previously powerless groups (such as women, blacks, Chicanos, and Native Americans), whose exclusion from the culture's intellectual life influenced the kind of knowledge the culture obtained of the world—that is, what the culture called truth. In other words, the acknowledgment that discourse carries ideology, an acknowledgment that has turned our attention to those in control of the discipline's discourse, and of academic discourse in general, philosophically legitimates the courts' efforts to determine whether those in power are systematically excluding members of powerless groups from participating in the academic enterprise. Unfortunately, the character and value of a faculty member's research, which academic scholars are more capable of determining than judges, juries, or government bureaus, ceases to be at issue when society demands objective definition of scholarship.

In defining an individual's intellectual contribution to the culture by quantity of production rather than by quality of mind or value of publication (which require overtly subjective appraisal), the discipline has fostered a professional competition for publication and visibility that overrides almost all other purposes of the profession. In research universities, where the pressure to demonstrate productivity is generally more intense than in undergraduate colleges, faculty have little time to read each other's writing and little time to think about broad cultural issues; in fact we risk "getting behind" in our own disciplinary scholarship—at the expense of salary increases and promotions—when we venture to try to learn ways in which other disciplines understand the world. The same dualist subject/object orientation that established the canon of literary works and gave professors the task of interpreting those works as aesthetic objects characterizes our practices now: instead of thinking about a wide variety of matters related to human values, we devote our attention to a segment of the literary spectrum and exploit our mastery of it. As Ohmann says, a time may come "when each literary scholar knows only his *own* research, and we perish, not through entropy but through solipsism" (*English* 11).

Behind the move to objectify quality for purposes of evaluation are the Cartesian assumptions that objectivity is possible, that in decontextualizing the material under consideration the investigators may see it more clearly, and that the process of investigation does not influence the results obtained. In the same way that the academy has sought objectivity in the evaluation of research, it has sought objectivity in the evaluation of teaching. Although most research-oriented universities define faculty merit primarily by research productivity, increasingly promotion committees, department chairs, and deans, in considering tenure, promotions, salaries, and special awards, are looking at a candidate's teaching record. With the ostensible motives of giving faculty "feedback" on their teaching effectiveness, affording students the opportunity to report problems and to indicate approval, and using "objective"—supposedly fair—means to compare teachers, the academy has quantified teaching capability through student questionnaires and has thereby made faculty members conscious of the economic necessity of being popular with students. The academy has equated measurable levels of popularity with degrees of excellence in teaching. Yet by giving students influence over professors' teaching methods, materials, testing procedures, and standards of grading, the academy has built into its teaching a conservatism, for its democratic gesture of appealing to students' opinions inhibits professors' introduction into the classroom of new, potentially disturbing, ways of thinking.

In describing our discipline's structure I have simplified it somewhat in order to show how the Cartesian model of knowledge production in a capitalist society that defines worth by product has affected the study of literature. The new consciousness of systemic inequalities and the hope of legally rectifying injustices to make a more egalitarian society, which most of us desire, have made many faculty, administrators, and judges reluctant to distinguish ("discriminate") between academic "products" in terms of their value to society, because such a "subjective" judgment is susceptible to accusations of unfair discrimination against the scholar. Yet in a pluralistic, relativistic world, no totally "objective" value can be assigned to any intellectual contribution.

Should we, the intellectuals fortunate to have obtained an education in a world desperate for thinkers to solve serious problems, relinquish our responsibility to make judgments? On the other hand, can we continue to argue that only we academics may make academic judgments when we recognize the politics of various discourses, including our own? Can we continue to support the myth of the separation of the academy from society when academic physicists do Pentagon research and biologists accept large grants from pharmaceutical companies? Do we continue to allow a dualist, capitalist model to govern our practices when, increasingly, we acknowledge the ending of that paradigm? Do we continue to seek refuge in our areas of specialization from the pressing global problems that call for thoughtful cultural analysis?

Intellectuals of various disciplines now view the mechanistic model of reality as outmoded and increasingly dangerous to our survival as a human race, for in that model we failed to recognize, as Eugene Odum says, that "the environment of any organism serves as both a 'supply depot' and a 'house'" (*Crisis* 10). Nonetheless, in the discipline of literary study we are prolonging the effects of that mechanistic model in ignoring our "house" (our society) in our professional practices. We have established an incentive system that encourages us to write only to each other; we have isolated ourselves from the society that supports academics to think and to teach its young to think, to the point that, as I noted in the introductory chapter to this book, the public uses the phrase "That's academic" to mean "That's irrelevant."

So how do we rescue the humanities? Or, more important, how can the holohumanities help rescue a society in crisis, the society which is our "house"? Because we cannot continue to separate theory from practice, or discuss the culture's intellectual life as if it were distinguishable from its practical life, I would suggest a reorientation not only of our traditional philosophical postures but of our practices. Here are some steps to take (steps which many institutions have already initiated):

In professional practices:
• Deemphasize quantity of publication (in hiring, tenuring, promoting, and paying faculty) in order to focus on quality of writing and teaching. (Questions to ask, impossible as they may be to answer definitively, would include: Does this individual address major issues? What kind of contribution does this individual make to the culture? For whom may this research—now or in the future—be valuable?) This change, by allowing time and incentives for thought, would decrease the pressure to specialize on a narrow topic and to publish at a scheduled or competitive rate.
• For promotion, tenure, and periodic evaluation, ask candidates to provide statements regarding their teaching, their research goals, and the significance of their research. This practice would ensure candidates the opportunity to explain the value of perhaps esoteric work to colleagues unfamiliar with their fields or their approaches.
• Establish interdisciplinary concept-oriented conferences and journals; and provide travel support to such conferences regardless of whether the scholar delivers a paper. In collaborating with scholars from other disciplines, we would be exchanging not facts or isolated observations but methods and approaches for the

making of order. One side effect of this interaction among the disciplines could be a decrease in jargon intelligible only to specialists in given fields; another side effect could be a decrease in numbers of scholarly papers, of regional conferences, and of journals.

In undergraduate and graduate teaching:
• Shift emphasis from interpretation of canonical works in isolation from political, economic, and scientific events to interpretation of a variety of texts. Thus we could more fully integrate "literature" into the culture's general discourse.
• Develop more team-taught interdisciplinary courses in which students see two or more ways of interpreting phenomena in relation to each other, bringing together not only literature and art, for example, but also literature and physics and history, or literature and political science (so that they may learn, as Saussure said, that the point of view generates its object). Not only the students but also the faculty would thus become educated in the approaches of other disciplines.
• Teach interdisciplinary concept-oriented courses (such as "the Industrial Revolution," "the systems model," or "subjectivism").
• Encourage interdisciplinary "majors" and interdisciplinary graduate programs.
• Increase foreign language requirements to facilitate the understanding and tolerance of people's differences, in the interest of global community.

In academic structure:
• Facilitate (perhaps through interdisciplinary centers and institutes) the interaction of professors from different disciplines in research and teaching.

The premise of the suggestions for our evaluation procedures is that there is no such thing as "objectivity," that, in Fish's words, "interpretation is the only game in town" (355). The related premise of the suggestions for integrating literature into other discourse is that meaning is contextual.

If we believe that all knowledge is interpretation, then in our professional practices we should act upon our theory and accept responsibility for evaluating (interpreting) scholarly work. Of course not all human beings are competent interpreters of all texts, since one's construction of a text's meaning depends upon one's knowledge of the text's context, one's expectations, and one's ideological presuppositions; therefore, we must seek to designate (to the extent possible) appropriate interpretive bodies, according to their participation in the appropriate "interpretive communities," to evaluate research. (I am assuming that most professors, given this responsibility, will strive to be fair.) As Fish says, "Communication occurs within situations and . . . to be in a situation is already to be in possession of (or to be possessed by) a structure of assumptions, of practices understood to be relevant in relation to purposes and goals that are already in place; and it is within the assumption of these purposes and goals that any utterance is *immediately* heard" (318). Only by abandoning fallacious objectivity (the present incentive structure) within the university can we reassert our own authority to interpret academic accomplishment; and then we must educate the public to the fallaciousness of the equation of objectivity and impartiality.

The value to the culture of a scholar's research will hardly be indisputable. For the same reasons that, as I have shown in other chapters, some texts have been canonized and others neglected or forgotten, reasons pertaining to ideology and social structure, some scholarly work will be deemed more academically or culturally valuable than other scholarly work; and arguments over these matters will likely involve the political positions of both the evaluators and the scholars being evaluated. So I am simply proposing that we subordinate consideration of quantity to the question of value when we assess research, in order to make room in the profession for thinkers attempting to address major issues, who may not be publishing on a schedule comparable to that of their colleagues specializing in fairly narrow areas.

If we abandon a belief in objectivity, we must redefine the principle of "academic freedom," for the public and for ourselves, in terms of contextual value. The discipline—and the academic world generally—cannot use the notion of academic independence from politics to support academic-evaluation-by-academics after it has shown society's intellectual activity to be inseparable from its political activity. Such inconsistency undermines the persuasiveness of academic freedom as a *practical* principle crucial to a culture's intellectual advancement. However, if we define the principle in terms of the culture's need for relative freedom of thought in higher education, from which would follow the logic of contextual evaluation, then we can justify philosophically an argument that public interference in individual academic decisions is usually not beneficial to society.

By employing Fish's concept of "interpretive communities" the discipline can argue that only the pertinent interpretive community of scholars can interpret scholarly contributions and academic documents appropriately, for within that community scholars share an awareness of what constitutes new and valuable thinking. Without context, a text is meaningless: to remove a text (a curriculum vitae, a letter of evaluation, a collection of scholarly articles, a book, a report of a scientific experiment, for example) from the intellectual discourse in which it was written and to introduce it into the courtroom to a jury unacquainted with the text's context is to render it meaningless, assessable only in terms of numbers of pages, to be interpreted by judge and jurors according to their own experiences of what those words mean. Moreover, to grant the public authority over the personnel of academic units, and thereby over the content of courses and over the critical approaches employed in teaching and research, is equally inappropriate and, in the long run, as dangerous to free inquiry as outright censorship.

Yet here again we encounter the problem I have addressed in other chapters regarding the canon: Who are the scholars who constitute that "pertinent interpretive community"? Until recently, white males governed the profession and determined—with presumably the best of intentions—the nature of scholarly discourse; after laws forbidding racial and sexual discrimination brought women and nonwhites into positions of power, laws which affected hiring and promotion procedures in the academy, new kinds of scholarly discourse (such as nondisciplinary explorations of values, autobiographical styles of social critique) came to be appreciated as valuable. The circularity would seem to preclude fairness in any evaluation of research: because it is federal law that mandates fairness in hiring and promotion, the courtroom seems an appropriate place for its determination; however, because juries lack the competence to judge the worth of scholarly publication, the courtroom seems an inappropriate place. Thus the recommendation for preserving academic-evaluation-by-academics is perhaps suitable for implementation only after society has achieved a self-consciousness with respect to "equal opportunity" and after the academy has achieved a general awareness of the relationship of knowledge to power. Whether that time has come is debatable. But, at the end of the twentieth century, the practical advantages of assuming that academics constitute the most appropriate interpretive community for evaluating thought outweigh the disadvantages in the promotion of intellectual freedom (itself only an ideal) in higher education.

For that reason we must retain the institution of tenure, for without tenure for established researchers and teachers, we have no opportunity for freedom of thought and expression for either scholars or students. But since we can no longer contend that our scholarly activities—whether they be in literature, history, or biology—imply no ideology, since we can no longer contend that the academy can operate free of political pressures, and since we can no longer believe that truth is not socially influenced, we must claim academic freedom and tenure on the relativistic grounds of social value: it is for the continued health of the country that our society should grant us, its academic intellectuals, the freedom to seek understanding of the world, to publish the results of our research, and to teach what we know to our students.

The question will inevitably arise: How can our society eliminate unfair discrimination against women and powerless minorities, discrimination supported by the Cartesian paradigm, without subscribing to supposedly objective means of evaluation? By returning authority to academic interpretive communities—to departments or divisions—to make promotion and tenure decisions according to subjective evaluation of a candidate's intellectual contribution to the culture, do we not license our colleagues to vote according to arbitrary affections and aversions? Do we not then permit those in authority to maintain their authority by not admitting to their ranks those who might challenge them? Do we not thereby unintentionally maintain the dualist paradigm that feminists and minorities have criticized?

The problem is particularly acute now, when we are still in the midst of the shift between the dualist paradigm and the holistic, when we have revealed the social injustices built into the structure of the old paradigm but have not yet achieved the egalitarianism implicit in the new. Having provided an extensive critique of the means whereby the (white, male) academic establishment has (unconsciously) enforced values that preserved its authority in the discipline of literary study, scholars devoted to rectifying the situation have found "objective" comparison of publication and teaching records to be the only means offered by the current political system to integrate women and minorities into the academy.

Yet to subscribe to this practice within the disciplinary structure of higher education carries not only the disadvantage of philosophical inconsistency on the part of those criticizing the dualist model for its support of oppression but also the difficulty of fitting nondisciplinary research into disciplinary categories. Feminist scholars who disregard disciplinary boundaries in the effort to expose hidden ideological presuppositions of the culture's discourse may encounter the objection that such research is not "academic": it does not meet standard disciplinary criteria—of methodology, of subject matter, of style—for acceptance as sound scholarly work. Further difficulties arise. The publication of such nondisciplinary research in interdisciplinary feminist journals, for example, or journals dedicated to black studies or Chicano studies, may be considered less of an accomplishment, and therefore less deserving of serious attention, than publication in widely distributed discipline-oriented journals. This occurs because senior scholars within the discipline, until recently, have not been associated with the new radical journals; and the prestigious disciplinary journals, until recently, have had few women or members of minority groups on their editorial boards. Resistance to nontraditional research is inevitable: how can an academic community accept as valuable scholarship that writing which challenges not only its values and assumptions but also the very style of its research? What is remarkable—and to its credit—is the extent to which the academy does, in its structure, protect the development of revolutionary ideas, as demonstrated by the institutionalization of women's studies programs.

However, feminist scholarship has begun to affect the discipline's concept of research; and through its critique of the values implicit in Cartesian dualism, it has demonstrated a holistic approach to learning. In recognizing that the division of knowledge into disciplines has inhibited an examination of the culture's values, women scholars have shown the need to branch out from our discipline's traditional subject matter, the literary canon, to understand texts contextually. Now few literary scholars can afford to ignore feminist research, because it has fundamentally changed the landscape, and before long few scholars of any discipline will be able successfully to pursue traditional disciplinary research in ignorance of the feminist critique of Cartesianism. Before long, "feminist research" will not be a subcategory of "research." Feminists have extended Heisenberg's lesson, that what we can know of the world is relative to our methods of investigation, to encompass the ideology of the investigators: what we know of the world is relative both to the methods of investigation and to the values and interests of those particular people in charge of the investigation. A thorough exploration of this lesson will bring about, I hope, an egalitarian society.

The critique of objectivity should lead to a reformation of the curriculum. To avoid promulgating values that many believe function to oppress certain classes, we should concentrate on training students in critical thinking with respect to all kinds of texts; we would thereby avoid unresolvable political quarrels regarding the constitution of the canon, quarrels elicited by the Arnoldian faith in the universal value of "the best which has been thought and said in the world." In teaching students to look to a text's source and to a text's context when interpreting a text—that is, by alerting students to ideological implications of texts—the holohumanities would develop in students a skepticism beneficial to a democratic electorate. Citizens capable of critical thinking are less susceptible to coercion from powerful groups (of whatever kind—political, commercial, religious) than are believers in a fixed body of knowledge or believers in a single approach to learning. We would also, by this shift in orientation, return literature to the world of morality and politics, since we would no longer treat literature as intrinsically superior to and distinct from other kinds of texts of "the real world."

However, the implementation of a contextual approach to literature would require some reorientation of the discipline's practices and purposes for both undergraduate and graduate teaching, a reorientation that many liberal arts colleges have already begun in "humanities" programs. (In fact, I am primarily concerned here with undergraduate courses, because the undergraduate curriculum influences to a large extent the values of society's educated; and graduate courses are already showing the influence of interdisciplinary critical theory.) The prevailing assumption, manifested in such textbooks as *The Norton Anthology of American Literature* and Macmillan's *Literature of the Western World*, is not only that literary works constitute the primary subject matter of the discipline but also that "coverage" of the field, achieved by a representative sampling of a wide variety of works, is the aim of an introductory course. As long as the discipline retains as its primary purpose the interpretation of literature alone, and as long as it retains textbooks anthologizing literature alone, it will perpetuate the disagreement over what constitutes "literature." Therefore, in order to demonstrate the interrelatedness of texts and events, we must relinquish both the goal of representative sampling (an academic effect of the dualist belief in an objectively definable external reality) and the practice of teaching only (or mainly) literary works in "literature" classes. Instead, in undergraduate concept-oriented courses we could gather together a wide variety of texts in service of understanding the history of a particular idea and learning to interpret and write about texts in relation to that idea. Ultimately, if we are to institute this approach for undergraduate classes throughout junior colleges, colleges, and universities, we must make available new textbooks, textbooks that integrate literary works, pertinent documents, articles from other disciplines, reports of relevant events, and, perhaps, illustrations from the visual arts.

How would such an approach work for an undergraduate comparative literature course on "The Breakdown of Dualism," for instance? The syllabus could include not only such literature as Pirandello's *Six Characters in Search of an Author*, Stein's "Picasso," Woolf's *The Waves*, Breton's Surrealist poetry (plus his "Surrealist Manifesto"), Sartre's *Nausea*, Queneau's *Exercises in Style*, and Calvino's *Invisible Cities* (all standard works for a twentieth-century course), but also Nietzsche's parable of "The Madman," Freud's "A Note on the Unconscious in Psychoanalysis," Dewey's "The Influence of Darwinism on Philosophy," a chapter from Heisenberg's *The Physicist's Conception of Nature*, articles by the Odums on ecology and Capra on contemporary physics, Wolfe's *The Painted Word*, and a selection of illustrations from the visual arts—impressionism, cubism, and abstract expressionism in painting, and so on. (I have listed, it may be pointed out, primarily canonized literature, thus apparently contradicting arguments I have made elsewhere regarding the ideology implicit in the formation of our canon; however, my purpose here is to provide an example of a syllabus, for which reason I have given titles familiar to most members of the profession.) The course would aim to teach the interpretation of texts in relation to each other: it would aim to instill in students an ability to think and to write critically about texts of all kinds.

Opponents to the establishment of concept-oriented courses for undergraduates may argue, perhaps with some justification, that the substitution of them for survey courses in the undergraduate curriculum may deprive students of a wide-ranging knowledge of literature, leaving nonliterature majors with only an acquaintance of a few particular themes in Western civilization. The question to consider, however, is whether survey courses actually accomplish that ideal, or whether instead they endow students with knowledge of only a smattering of literary works which few can relate to texts they meet in other courses. Most faculty would agree that few undergraduates are able to connect modern literature with science, for example, or with the history of American politics; students read *The Waste Land* with little thought about the effect of Darwin on the culture, or of Einstein, or of Picasso, or of World War I, even when they are simultaneously taking courses in biology, physics, art, and history. Furthermore, after a survey course of Western literature, many students are incapable even of relating the various poems, plays, and novels to each other. And students encounter among their professors specialists in diverse fields who do not believe it their responsibility to associate their subject matter with that of their colleagues across campus.

An argument in favor of the concept approach would be that its orientation toward contextual interpretation would provide students with training in critical thinking and with frameworks for the organization of information. The inclusion of nonliterary texts in "literature" courses would by no means imply a neglect of "literature": instead it would encourage students (and faculty) to see the relevance of literary texts to the social world, for it would render more visible literature's powers of persuasion; it would render more visible intention and effect. Such an approach would translate our century's philosophical recognition that our knowledge of the world depends upon our questions and our viewpoint into pedagogy: students' knowledge of literary works (and other texts) would be relative to the particular issue they investigated in the course. However, because the course would center upon a particular issue, students would be likely to understand and remember what they studied, having a means to order the texts.

The academy has already incorporated into itself at least one integrative discipline in the humanities (women's studies) devoted to the reconstruction of the culture's order of knowledge and perhaps its social structure. Programs in women's studies, black studies, and Chicano studies have all offered interdisciplinary courses since their beginnings, for the "fields" originated with an awareness that disciplinary courses omitted material necessary for the understanding of noncanonical texts. Teaching new ways of interpreting material, professors in these programs have produced citizens eager to reform social structures and scholars eager to revamp literary history. To the criticism that they have turned research and teaching into political activism, they may reply that all discourse implies an ideology of some sort and that they are simply declaring openly their purposes and interests. Although their argument raises for many faculty questions of academic freedom and academic propriety, such that the programs have frequently brought controversy to institutions, their success in arming students with an ability to analyze texts (albeit with a particular political purpose) cannot be ignored. Other humanistic programs of study, other integrative disciplines, other interdisciplinary or nondisciplinary courses may obtain similar success in advancing students' analytical abilities by teaching modes of interpretation and models for organizing phenomena.

The discipline is changing—in part as a consequence of the civil rights movement, the Vietnam War, and the feminist movement, all of which have helped to bring about a general dissatisfaction with the discipline's traditional assumptions and practices. Soon the children of the sixties—who demonstrated, in protest against the military-industrial establishment twenty years ago, a desire for a more egalitarian society—will dominate our profession, if not our whole society; and—though I may be accused of utopianism—I would say that this generation, thanks to the pioneering feminists and civil rights workers who brought society's attention to its oppression of the powerless, is more *consciously* devoted than previous generations to total integration. As Thomas Kuhn argues in *The Structure of Scientific Revolutions* regarding the institutionalization of a paradigm, a new model takes over when those new to the profession who see things differently from their older colleagues, the relatively young who have not invested years of their lives in the older way of making order, obtain maturity and power. Women and members of minority groups are serving now in the prestigious and powerful positions of journal editors, MLA committee chairs, department chairs, chairs of promotion committees, and academic administrators, positions that institutionalize values; a woman, Phyllis Franklin, has become executive director of the Modern Language Association. So the problem that women and minorities have faced in obtaining a voice in the culture's discourse and in the profession may actually disappear—in a generation.

The end of Cartesian reductionism may eventually mean a shift in the definition of all the disciplines whereby contextual understanding of phenomena will be implicit in the constitution of their subject matter. The new holohumanist should be able to relate his or her knowledge of a particular field to the larger picture; he or she may know well not necessarily a particular set of data, but rather a particular method or approach to understanding events in context, an approach enabling him or her to give order to diverse data in a rapidly changing world; or a particular period of history—its literary texts, its political documents, its economic structure, its scientific model of reality; or a particular mode of expression. Thus the holohumanist may resemble what in the Cartesian model appeared to be a generalist, a thinker capable of synthesizing many kinds of information generated in many fields. In the pluralism implicit in the holohumanities—a pluralism born of the assumption that in a nondualist reality "coverage" of a field is impossible, a bygone illusion—we shall feel encouraged to focus on whatever we find most important and most interesting to us, for we shall be judged on the quality of our thinking and of our writing and on its value to the intellectual community of which we are part.

The shift in orientation from "literature" to methods of investigation, modes of interpretation, and ways of integrating the particular into the larger system will not mean abandoning the culture's accumulated knowledge of a field; nor will it mean—in the study of a "literary" text, for example—neglecting the peculiarities of the text or the particularities of the text's period of history. To the contrary: if meaning is contextual, then intelligent interpretation of the text will entail a thorough understanding of the text's context (social, political, economic, scientific, and so forth), a context that is diachronic as well as synchronic. For holohumanities, the reorientation simply means a change *in emphasis* from literature as the discipline's objectified subject matter to contextual interpretation and an inclusion in the discipline of many kinds of writing that literary scholars formerly ignored. Holohumanistic scholars will continue the practice of becoming better acquainted with the texts in one period of history than in another, or with one kind of text than another, or with the texts of one or two nations—the practice we have called specialization—but in resistance to the reductionist habit of isolating the object of attention from its context and with self-consciousness regarding method. Holohumanists will accept a responsibility for synthesizing, for explaining the political implications of ideas, and for communicating such knowledge to the public.

In the past several years thoughtful academics across the country have pointed to the need to continue education for the "out-of-school adult"; but it is not enough to offer the out-of-school adult simply new courses or conferences for "life-long learning." Holohumanists in particular, concerned not only with scholarly issues in our areas of specialization but also with political and ethical issues affecting our nation, must occasionally write for the public at large, educating people outside our fields when we find ourselves in the position to do so, bringing to bear on the problems of the day whatever special knowledge we may have that we believe pertinent. Our nation's quality of life depends on the extent to which we intellectuals help educate the whole of society—everybody who reads newspapers or watches television. In teaching students and the public that ideas have consequences, we shall be engaged in holistic education. The breakdown of the spirit/matter opposition, with its privileging of spirit, brings an end to the dichotomies of liberal arts/utilitarian sciences, science/technology, scholarship/journalism, and academy/public, as well as research/teaching.

The desire for many of these modifications to our traditional disciplinary practices is already "in the air" in the humanities, but the continued connection of salary and rank to academic product retards their implementation. As long as administrators evaluate faculty from different disciplines on basically the same product-oriented model, which they do with the motive of impartiality, then our discipline will be product-oriented, geared to specialization, and irrelevant to the interests of many Americans.

In 1870 Noah Porter, in opposition to scientific specialization, wrote:

> The theory of education, after which a curriculum of study has been prescribed, has been, that certain studies (among which the classics and mathematics are prominent) are best fitted to prepare a man for the most efficient and successful discharge of public duty. By "public duty" we do not mean merely professional duty, but duty in that relatively commanding position, which a thoroughly cultured man is fitted to occupy. By a thoroughly cultured man we mean a man who has been trained to know himself in his constitution, his duties, and his powers; to know society in its history and institutions, its literature and art; and to know nature in its developments and scientific relations. (92–93)

The conservative Porter abhorred what he perceived to be the atheism of Darwinian science, and he therefore advocated preserving the traditional liberal arts curriculum as good mental discipline which, when combined with religious teaching, would "exclude and counteract the atheistic tendencies of much of modern science, literature, and culture" (224). With the establishment of science in the colleges and universities, literary scholars forsook the goal of preparing students to be good citizens, and by the end of the nineteenth century they had distinguished literature from moral concerns, to teach (in Bradley's words) "poetry for poetry's sake." Perhaps, now that critics have explored the discipline's heretofore little-noticed ideology, now that critics have pointed out heretofore little-noticed sexism and racism in the traditional literary canon, now that critics have called attention to the inseparability of the culture's intellectual life from its political, we should return to the education philosophy of developing mental discipline (redefined as critical thinking) in students. However, we would do so not with Porter's assumption that such training would combat atheism, but rather with the purpose of developing good citizens capable of *critical* thinking, capable of exploring texts for their ethical implications, capable, therefore, of combatting coercion by any powerful group. Holohumanities, modified from a discipline of literary study oriented toward a subject matter to a discipline oriented toward the contextual interpretation of texts (among which will be "great literature") and toward the acquisition of writing skills—that is, reoriented from object to process—may thereby recover the position of centrality in higher education that the humanities once enjoyed.

As the culture eventually discards the dualist suppositions that only the specialist in a particular subject matter is qualified to solve problems, that the literary scholar is capable of intelligent analysis of literature alone, and that the poet or novelist is competent only in the techniques of imaginative writing, the new holohumanist will be appreciated by a technologically complex society that needs intelligent, widely read thinkers to articulate its problems, to reveal implicit values in its past and present discourse, to consider ethical implications of political, technological, and scientific events, and to help provide direction for its development. By reintegrating the poet into politics, we reintegrate ourselves as well.

Notes

Introduction

1. In recent years the question of the definition of literature has arisen again among critics with various relativist approaches who are examining the institution of literature in relation to other cultural institutions. See in particular Richard Ohmann, *English in America* (1976), Raymond Williams, *Marxism and Literature* (1977), Leslie Fiedler, *What Was Literature?* (1982), Terry Eagleton, *Literary Theory* (1983), William Cain, *The Crisis in Criticism* (1984), and Gerald Graff, *Professing Literature* (1987).

In "Mimesis and Contemporary French Theory," Mihai Spariosu writes:

> What is treated as literature in one age may become science in a different age, while scientific stretches of discourse may in turn come to be regarded as literature. In Western culture literature has, at least since Plato, acted as a differential principle for other stretches of discourse. By openly displaying its fictionality, it has allowed other linguistic constructs, such as history, natural science, philosophy, ethics, religion, politics, etc., to be invested with the authority of knowledge-truth. (99)

2. See Carolyn G. Heilbrun's article "The Profession and Society, 1958–83" for a discussion of the profession of literary study during this period. According to Heilbrun: "To question the role of women in society was obviously to question the authority of all those who spoke for or excused women's continuing subjugation. And so the women's movement in the 1960s unquestionably gained strength from another profound change: the collapse of faith in the honesty of our political and institutional leaders, indeed, of faith in the dominant institutions themselves" (412).

1. Dualism and the Concept of Literature

1. I am indebted to Marshall McLuhan and Father Walter Ong for the orientation of this book: McLuhan and Ong have shown Cartesian dualism to be a consequence of print literacy, and I am attempting to show the relationship of the discipline of literary study to the dualist paradigm.

133

2. See also Sir Philip Sidney's *The Defense of Poesy*, where he writes:

Neither let it be deemed too saucy a comparison to balance the highest point of man's wit
with the efficacy of nature, but rather give right honor to the Heavenly Maker of that maker
[the poet], who, having made man to His own likeness, set him beyond and over all the
works of that second nature, which in nothing he shows so much as in poetry, when with the
force of a divine breath he brings things forth far surpassing her doings. . . .

. . . Poesy therefore is an art of imitation, for so Aristotle terms it in the word *mimesis*,
that is to say a representing, counterfeiting, or figuring forth (to speak metaphorically, a
speaking picture) with this end, to teach and delight. (10, 11)

2. Dualism and "Culture"

1. See Park Honan's *Matthew Arnold: A Life* for extensive discussions of Arnold's
appreciation of Newman. According to Honan,

There isn't a leading conception of Matthew Arnold's about culture, the nature of criticism,
philistinism and liberalism, or the relation between poetry and religion that fails to reveal a
Newmanic tincture—though he had a magpie's ability to pick up bits and pieces from everywhere, to fill out conceptions in his essays, and he may have culled from texts that influenced Newman. What the preacher offered was an illustration of a mental attitude—delicate
and flexible, discriminating and urbane—that suggested all that a critical manner might be.
(61)

2. For a succinct discussion of the implications for human "nature" of the loss of
belief in a God, see Sartre's "Existentialism":

Atheistic existentialism . . . states that if God does not exist, there is at least one being in
whom existence precedes essence, a being who exists before he can be defined by any concept, and that this being is man, or, as Heidegger says, human reality. What is meant here
by saying that existence precedes essence? It means that, first of all, man exists, turns up,
appears on the scene, and, only afterwards, defines himself. If man, as the existentialist con-
ceives him, is indefinable, it is because at first he is nothing. Only afterward will he be
something, and he himself will have made what he will be. Thus, there is no human nature,
since there is no God to conceive it. (15)

See also Derrida's "Structure, Sign, and Play in the Discourse of the Human Sciences" for a discussion of the implications for "intrinsic meaning" of the loss of belief
in a God:

From then on it was probably necessary to begin to think that there was no center, that the
center could not be thought in the form of a being-present, that the center had no natural
locus, that it was not a fixed locus but a function, a sort of non-locus in which an infinite
number of sign-substitutions came into play. This moment was that in which language invaded the universal problematic; that in which, in the absence of a center or origin, everything became discourse—provided we can agree on this word—that is to say, when

everything became a system where the central signified, the original or transcendental signified, is never absolutely present outside a system of differences. The absence of the transcendental signified extends the domain and the interplay of signification *ad infinitum*. (249)

3. Science, the Humanities, and Higher Education

1. In 1909, in a lecture titled "The Influence of Darwinism on Philosophy" given
in a series on "Charles Darwin and His Influence on Science" at Columbia University,
John Dewey recognized *On the Origin of Species* as occasioning a major alteration of
the means by which the culture conceived of reality:

> The conception of . . . species, a fixed form and final cause, was the central principle of
> knowledge as well as of nature. Upon it rested the logic of science. Change as change is
> mere flux and lapse; it insults intelligence. Genuinely to know is to grasp a permanent end
> that realizes itself through changes, holding them thereby within the metes and bounds of
> fixed truth. Completely to know is to relate all special forms to their one single end and
> good: pure contemplative intelligence. Since, however, the scene of nature which directly
> confronts us is in change, nature as directly and practically experienced does not satisfy the
> conditions of knowledge. . . .
>
> . . . The Darwinian principle of natural selection cut straight under this philosophy. . . .
> . . . [In the intellectual transformation effected by the Darwinian logic] [i]nterest shifts
> from the wholesale essence back of special changes to the question of how special changes
> serve and defeat concrete purposes; shifts from an intelligence that shaped things once for all
> to the particular intelligences which things are even now shaping; shifts from an ultimate
> goal of good to the direct increments of justice and happiness that intelligent administration
> of existent conditions may beget and that present carelessness or stupidity will destroy or
> forego. (*Influence* 6, 11, 15)

2. See Dewey's chapter "Changed Conceptions of the Ideal and the Real" in *Reconstruction in Philosophy* for an extended discussion of the implications of the distinct modes of knowing: contemplation and experimentation. According to Dewey,

> The function of study and learning of philosophy is, as Plato put it, to convert the eye of the
> soul from dwelling contentedly upon the images of things, upon the inferior realities that are
> born and that decay, and to lead it to the intuition of supernal and eternal Being. Thus the
> mind of the knower is transformed. It becomes assimilated to what it knows.
>
> Through a variety of channels, especially Neo-Platonism and St. Augustine, these ideas
> found their way into Christian theology; and great scholastic thinkers taught that the end of
> man is to know True Being, that knowledge is contemplative, that True Being is pure Imma-
> terial Mind, and to know it is Bliss and Salvation. While this knowledge cannot be achieved
> in this stage of life nor without supernatural aid, yet so far as it is accomplished it assimi-
> lates the human mind to the divine essence and so constitutes salvation. Through this taking
> over of the conception of knowledge as Contemplative into the dominant religion of Europe,
> multitudes were affected who were totally innocent of theoretical philosophy. There was be-

queathed to generations of thinkers as an unquestioned axiom the idea that knowledge is intrinsically a mere beholding or viewing of reality—the spectator conception of knowledge. So deeply engrained was this idea that it prevailed for centuries after the actual progress of science had demonstrated that knowledge is power to transform the world, and centuries after the practice of effective knowledge had adopted the method of experimentation. (111–12)

3. Wellek and Warren, writing *Theory of Literature* in 1942, indicated clearly their preference for intrinsic approaches:

> Though the "extrinsic" study may merely attempt to interpret literature in the light of its social context and its antecedents, in most cases it becomes a "causal" explanation, professing to account for literature, to explain it, and finally to reduce it to its origins (the "fallacy of origins"). . . .
>
> . . . The natural and sensible starting-point for work in literary scholarship is the interpretation and analysis of the works of literature themselves. After all, only the works themselves justify all our interest in the life of an author, in his social environment and the whole process of literature. But, curiously enough, literary history has been so preoccupied with the setting of a work of literature that its attempts at an analysis of the works themselves have been slight in comparison with the enormous efforts expended on the study of environment. (73, 139)

4. In 1844 Darwin elaborated his theory of natural selection in a long essay which he refrained from publishing because of the religious controversy he knew it would precipitate. When Alfred Russel Wallace sent him a scientific paper in 1858 outlining a theory of natural selection practically identical to his, Darwin published a joint paper with Wallace in the Journal of the Linnean Society, "On the Tendency of Species to Form Varieties; and On the Perpetuation of Varieties and Species by Natural Means of Selection," and then went on to publish his own work, *On the Origin of Species*, the following year.

5. Louis Agassiz had written: "The history of the earth proclaims its Creator. It tells us that the object and the term of creation is man. He is announced in nature from the first appearance of organized beings; and each important modification in the whole series of these beings is a step towards the definitive term of the development of organic life" (quoted in Ruse 97).

6. Asa Gray wrote:

> From certain incidental expressions at the close of the volume, taken in connection with the motto adopted from Whewell, we judge it probable that our author regards the whole system of nature as one which had received at its first formation the impress of the will of its Author, foreseeing the varied yet necessary laws of its action throughout the whole of its existence, ordaining when and how each particular of the stupendous plan should be realized in effect, and—with Him to whom to will is to do—in ordaining doing it. Whether profoundly philosophical or not, a view maintained by eminent philosophical physicists and theologians . . . will hardly be denounced as atheism. (Wilson 35)

7. As Richard Hofstadter has shown, though the liberal arts dominated the college curriculum before the Civil War, both geology and chemistry were taught, but with little laboratory work and in such a way as not to challenge *Genesis*. Mathematics, one of the original "liberal arts," served to instill mental discipline (19–20).

8. Most of the early American colleges were established to train ministers. Harvard had as its primary purpose the advancement and perpetuation of learning for the education of ministers. The charter of William and Mary, the second American college, stated as its purpose that "the church of Virginia may be furnished with a seminary of the Ministers of the Gospel, and that the youth may be piously educated in good letters and manners, and that the Christian faith may be propagated amongst the Western Indians to the glory of Almighty God" (quoted in Hofstadter 4). The third college, Yale, founded by ministers in 1701, was to be a school "wherein youth may be instructed in the arts & sciences, who through the blessing of Almighty God may be fitted for publick employment, both in church and civil state" (quoted in Hofstadter 4). Princeton was formed by Presbyterians in 1746, Columbia (King's College) by Episcopalians in 1754, Brown by Baptists in 1764, Rutgers (Queen's College) by members of the Reformed Church in 1766, and Dartmouth by a Congregational clergyman wishing to bring Christianity to the Indians in 1769 (Hofstadter 3–4).

9. J. B. Mozley, professor of divinity and canon of Christ Church, Oxford, wrote in an article for *Popular Science Monthly* published in 1872:

> As languages, French and German (especially the former) are less powerful instruments of training, for the abler boys, than Latin and Greek. As literatures—that is, as summing up the whole thought and history of a nation—they would, if properly managed, be much more powerful instruments (in proportion to the much greater variety of modern life as compared with ancients), and are, besides, much more important for us to know. (399)

10. See Edward Shils for further discussion of the implications of specialization for the academic world in the late nineteenth century.

> One of the principal elements of the German tradition—and a major factor in the triumph of the university within the American order of learning—was the emergence of specialization as a requirement of scientific and scholarly achievement. Systematic training in the universities, especially at the postgraduate level, was more conducive to specialization than was the self-education of the amateur. The specialized academic was in regular contact with his specialized colleagues and he was expected to demonstrate both a detailed mastery of numerous minute details and an acquaintance with a large number of publications dealing with these details. . . . The need to achieve, manifested in the desire for recognition, loyalty to a department and university, personal ambition, and the scientific ethos all pressed for publication as rapidly as possible. The more productive specialists became, the more imperative specialization became—it was impossible for any one person to master more than a narrow sector of the expanding body of scientific literature. . . .
>
>   . . . The growing conviction that "truth always lies in the details" meant that the details had to be explored with increasing thoroughness. As the word dilettante became a term of

scorn, the American academic order increasingly turned to the German model of *Fach-menschentum*. . . . There was a stern moral overtone to specialization. It meant no trifling, no self-indulgence. It was unsympathetic to false pride and omniscience. In sum, specialization was consistent with the secularized Protestant puritanism of the quarter century preceding World War I. (31–32)

11. Josiah Parsons Cooke, professor of chemistry at Harvard, acknowledged frankly that there would be a difference in class between those students who would choose a classical education and those students who would choose to obtain a scientific education in a separate scientific school. In an 1883 *Popular Science Monthly* article arguing for the right of scientists to direct the training of their own "men," he wrote:

> Although we think that there are many students now coming to us through the classical schools who would run a better chance of becoming useful men if they were trained from the beginning in a different way, yet such is the social prestige of the old classical schools and of the old classical culture that, whatever new relations might be established, the class of students which alone we now have would, I am confident, all continue to come through the old channels. . . .
>
>   . . . We look, then, for no change in the classical schools. Our only expectation is to affiliate the college with a wholly different class of schools, which will send us a wholly different class of students, with wholly different aims, and trained according to a wholly different method. At the outset we shall look to the best of our New England high-schools for a limited supply of scientific students, and hope by constant pressure to improve the methods of teaching in these schools, as our literary colleagues have within ten years vastly improved the methods in the classical schools. (4–5)

4. Dualism and the Canon

1. The New Critics, who received their name from John Crowe Ransom's 1941 book *The New Criticism*, and who included the Southerners Allen Tate, Cleanth Brooks, and Robert Penn Warren, among others, argued for the critical analysis of the literary work itself as more valuable to the study of literature than historical, biographical, or psychological scholarship. In a 1941 essay titled "Literature as Knowledge," Tate wrote: "We must return to, we must never leave, the poem itself. Its 'interest' value is a cognitive one; it is sufficient that here, in the poem, we get knowledge of a whole object" (48).

2. See both "The Death of the Author" and "From Work to Text" in Barthes's *Image-Music-Text* for a discussion of the difference between the concept of literary work and the concept of the "text." In the former essay Barthes writes:

> The work is caught up in a process of filiation. Are postulated: a *determination* of the work by the world (by race, then by History), a *consecution* of works amongst themselves, and a *conformity* of the work to the author. The author is reputed the father and the owner of his work: literary science therefore teaches *respect* for the manuscript and the author's declared

intentions, while society asserts the legality of the relation of author to work (the *"droit d'auteur"* or "copyright," in fact of recent date since it was only really legalized at the time of the French Revolution). As for the Text, it reads without the inscription of the Father. Here again, the metaphor of the Text separates from that of the work: the latter refers to the image of an *organism* which grows by vital expansion, by "development" (a word which is significantly ambiguous, at once biological and rhetorical); the metaphor of the Text is that of the *network*; if the Text extends itself, it is as a result of a combinatory systematic (an image, moreover, close to current biological conceptions of the living being). Hence no vital "respect" is due to the Text: it can be *broken* (which is just what the Middle Ages did with two nevertheless authoritative texts—Holy Scripture and Aristotle); it can be read without the guarantee of its father, the restitution of the inter-text paradoxically abolishing any legacy. (160–61)

3. I have quoted my own definition for "twentieth-century monism" from *Literary Relativity*.

In the absence of a God, a transcendent source of meaning for phenomena, both subject and object appear without "essence," and accordingly they become definable only in relation to each other. In such a universe, all things and events become definable only in relation to each other, with respect to their differences, in a system without center, without origin, and without *telos*. (18)

4. See Alvin C. Kibel's "The Canonical Text" for a history of the canon. According to Kibel:

Among the ancient Hebrews, a body of writings considered holy and subject to exegesis was clearly extant before the historical recognition of the canon, as many canonical texts themselves bear witness. Until the advent of canonization, however, interpretations important enough to be written down and repeatedly transcribed could be embedded at various points in the original text, which might then be recast to smooth out transitions—a process analogous to the composition of a modern text by a single author, whose secondary and tertiary revisions include new materials meant to elucidate the old. The practice of interpreting scripture, or midrash, is not a postbiblical phenomenon, but until the formation of an explicit canon, no essential distinction was observed between "primary" and "secondary" materials; indeed, recognition of the canon is coterminous with the historical advent of the secondary text, a new sort of writing which seeks neither to substitute for the primary text nor to add itself to the textual deposit wherein the primary is recorded. (243–44)

5. In the early thirties, before the publication of *Understanding Poetry*, the major poetry anthologies included *Lyric America: An Anthology of American Poetry, 1630–1930* (1930), edited by Alfred Kreymborg; *The New Poetry: An Anthology of Twentieth-Century Verse in English*, edited by Harriet Monroe and Alice Corbin Henderson; and the two volumes edited by Louis Untermeyer, which were the most widely used, *American Poetry: From the Beginning to Whitman* (1931) and *Modern American Poetry* (through the fifth edition in 1936) (B. Franklin, "English" 100–101). Untermeyer in the former volume grouped the poems according to their authors and then concluded with a section called "Appendices," which contained American Indian poetry, Spanish-colonial Verse, early American ballads, Negro spirituals, Negro social, "blues"

and work songs, "Negroid" melodies, cowboy songs and hobo harmonies, backwoods ballads, and city gutterals (*American Poetry* xxi-xxvi). Untermeyer included in this section of anonymous verse such songs as "Joshua Fit de Battle ob Jerico," "Nobody Knows de Trouble I See," "Ezekiel Saw de Wheel," "Old Folks at Home," "My Old Kentucky Home, Good-night," "Dixie," "The Lone Prairie," "My Horses Ain't Hungry," and "Frankie and Johnny," many of which were recorded in the folk song revival of the early 1960s. In the category of "Negroid" melodies, Untermeyer put those of Stephen Foster and Daniel Dacatur Emmett, both white men, whose songs "the Negroes adopted as their own" (751–52). In his introduction to the appendices Untermeyer wrote:

> One must regretfully conclude that the finest American folksongs of *native* origin are not those in the Anglo-Saxon tradition. They are the ritualistic American Indian dance-invoca-tions and love-songs—an oral literature that has defied assimilation—and the Negro Spir-ituals, which, with their mixture of exaltation and incongruous humor, are undoubtedly the most compelling. Beside these full-throated and fervid chants, even the tree-felling rhythms of the lumberjacks seem anemic. No resume can ignore these primitive and vital exhibits. (688–899)

In his *Modern American Poetry* he included poetry by numerous blacks—James Weldon Johnson, Paul Laurence Dunbar, Claude McKay, Jean Toomer, Langston Hughes, and Countee Cullen—as well as that of more than 35 women, in the 153 poets represented. His intention, set forth in the foreword to the fourth edition, was "to reflect the rise and fall of certain tendencies and to show, besides the presence of a few imposing figures, the emergence of many whose work, not impressive in mass, is interesting and even significant in detail" (v).

In their 1932 edition of *The New Poetry* Monroe and Henderson presented selec-tions of the poetry of 162 poets, of whom one-third were women.

6. *Understanding Poetry* included two or more poems by each of the follow-ing: Matthew Arnold; William Blake; Elizabeth Barrett Browning; Robert Brown-ing; William Cullen Bryant; Robert Burns; George Gordon, Lord Byron; Richard Crashaw; H.D.; Walter de la Mare; Emily Dickinson; John Donne; John Dryden; T.S. Eliot; Ralph Waldo Emerson; Robert Frost; Thomas Hardy; George Herbert; Robert Herrick; A. E. Housman; Ben Jonson; John Keats; Walter Savage Landor; Andrew Marvell; George Meredith; John Milton; Edgar Allan Poe; Alexander Pope; Sir Walter Ralegh; John Crowe Ransom; William Shakespeare; Percy Bysshe Shelley; Sir Philip Sidney; Edmund Spenser; Allen Tate; Alfred, Lord Tennyson; Henry Vaughan; William Wordsworth; William Butler Yeats.

7. In the first American poetry anthology, *American Poems, Selected and Original* (1793), its editor, Elihu Hubbard Smith, had aimed to preserve poems published in newspapers and periodicals that might otherwise have been lost and to build a literary tradition for the United States, which had just won its independence from Britain. Early nineteenth-century anthologies had sought, in addition to nationalistic poems,

those poems that provided moral instruction, imparting the view that American morality differed from European decadence; with this ideology they naturally excluded any writer whose poetry did not support the moral status quo. But after scholars had defined an American literature, anthologists, beginning with Charles A. Dana's *Household Book of Poetry* (1958) and including Ralph Waldo Emerson's *Parnassus* (1875), selected poems according to what they then believed were universal standards. In the last decades of the nineteenth century, the art-for-art's sake movement released poetry from any obligation to inspire morally and thus brought further changes to the developing canon: Walt Whitman finally achieved prominence in America when the British editor William Michael Rossetti included him in *American Poems: A Collection of Representative Verse* in 1872, after which Edmund Clarence Stedman put him into his *American Anthology, 1787–1900* (1900). According to Alan Golding, Stedman inverted the values determining canon selection by collecting poems that rebelled against rather than supported literary norms, poems that were innovative rather than conservative, and thus anticipated modernism (280–97).

In the eighteenth century, writers and scholars seeking to define an American literary tradition had looked to Europe for their models, because Native Americans did not provide any: "literature" meant writing, and "oral literature" seemed a contradiction in terms. When they did encounter native songs or chants, they characterized them as "natural," attributing them not to individuals but to tribes, as if to "nature" itself. With Romanticism, as literature came to mean particularly expressive or imaginative writing, rather than the whole of writing, and as "nature" became increasingly attractive, scholars began to translate Native American expression for its "natural" poetry. By 1907 collectors of Native song had published several anthologies, including Natalie Curtis's *The Indian Book*, containing music, poems, and short tribal narratives. And after World War I, in association with the left-wing demand for cultural pluralism, George W. Cronyn, who edited *The Path on the Rainbow* (1918), and Mary Austin, who provided its introduction, attempted to integrate Native American poetry into the canon (Krupat 310–17); Austin wrote: "It becomes appropriate and important that this collection of American Indian verse should be brought to public notice at a time when the whole instinctive movement of the American people is for a deeper footing in their native soil" (Cronyn xvii). But the proletariat-oriented scholars lost their battle to the New Critics in the late thirties, when with the desire to systematize the discipline scholars opted for a canon expressive of universal values and followed Eliot's conception of a single (European-American) literary "tradition," the latest works of which necessarily addressed the "timeless" concerns of the whole.

8. *Fifty Years of American Poetry*, the anniversary volume for the Academy of American Poets, for which Robert Penn Warren wrote the introduction, contained a poem by each of the chancellors, fellows, and award winners since the academy's founding in 1934 (126 poets in all), but included none by any of the black poets Untermeyer had presented in his 1930 edition.

9. See the introduction by Louis Kampf and Paul Lauter to the book they edited, titled *The Politics of Literature*, for a detailed account of the 1968 MLA meeting:

> Looking back at those events after two more conventions, and from a very different campus scene, what strikes us most about MLA 1968 was the amount of political and intellectual energy our organizing helped to release. Out of the seminar, initially on "Student Rebellions and the Teaching of Literature," a number of small groups emerged, including one on women. Two members of that group, occasional participants in Tactics meetings, tentatively proposed toward the end of the business meeting a sense of the body motion to establish a Commission on the Status of Women, which has proved one of the most significant instruments in pressuring for change in the profession and in the literary curriculum. . . .
>   . . . It may seem a hard prescription to propose that teachers of literature, trained by graduate school in detachment and privacy, should conceive as central to their *work* entering actively into political struggle. But one might consider that our classroom objective is to make literature a vital part of students' lives, rather than an antiquarian or formal study or a means of forcing them into feelings of "cultural deprivation." In other words, we want to change the relationship of students to literature in a classroom from that of passive consumption of culture to an active engagement with the emotions, ideas, politics, and sensibilities of writers and of others. (39, 44)

5. From Dualism to Holism

1. In his 1939 paper "The Relation of Habitual Thought and Behavior to Language" Whorf offers an explanation for the development of Western dualism which complements McLuhan's later emphasis on print as an influence on Cartesianism:

> From the form-plus-substance dichotomy the philosophical views most traditionally characteristic of the "Western world" have derived huge support. Here belong materialism, psychophysical parallelism, physics—at least in its traditional Newtonian form—and dualistic views of the universe in general. Indeed here belongs almost everything that is "hard, practical common sense." Monistic, holistic, and relativistic views of reality appeal to philosophers and some scientists, but they are badly handicapped in appealing to the "common sense" of the Western average man—not because nature herself refutes them (if she did, philosophers could have discovered this much), but because they must be talked about in what amounts to a new language. "Common sense," as its name shows, and "practicality" as its name does not show, are largely matters of talking so that one is readily understood. . . .
>   . . . Concepts of "time" and "matter" are not given in substantially the same form by experience to all men but depend upon the nature of the language or languages through the use of which they have been developed. (152, 158)

2. In arguing for a critical review of the departmental structure of higher education, Eugene Odum distinguishes between "interdisciplinary approaches" and "integrative disciplinary approaches":

A better first approach, I believe, is to encourage the emergence of programs and institutes that create a synthesis or that successfully integrate disciplines so as to match the level of societal problems. . . . Truly "integrative disciplinary approaches" should be given priority over "inter- or cross-disciplinary approaches" that make no effort to seek the synergism and new knowledge that often comes when knowledge and techniques of several conventional disciplines are combined. . . . For example, we view the modern field of ecology as not just a smattering of physical, biological, and social science, but as an essentially new effort emerging out of biology, but no longer restricted by its mother subject. Thus, ecologists now focus on the ecosystem (short for ecological system) which emphasizes not the separate study of man and nature, but the synergism and interaction between the two. ("Diversity" 11)

3. I believe that the adjectives *nondualistic, relativistic, holistic*, and *ecological* may all be applied to the paradigm succeeding Cartesian dualism. That paradigm is relativistic because no absolute frame of reference stabilizes meanings and values, holistic because meanings and definitions depend on the whole system (social and "natural" together), which is unbounded, and ecological because the integrative discipline of ecology provides a new model for understanding phenomena. In *Literary Relativity* I used the terms "relativistic monism" and "twentieth-century monism" to indicate the same paradigm.

4. While late twentieth-century theorists argue the untenability of the philosophical distinction between fiction and fact and while postmodernist writers blend fiction and criticism within their texts, all in opposition to a conservative academic establishment that maintains in its curriculum a separation of literature from history, television seizes upon the forms of fictional narration to present "fact"—in "docudramas" as well as in news programs—and the forms of factual narration to present fiction. Since television began to broadcast both "news" and "drama," and particularly since the Vietnam War, audiences have confused entertainment and verifiable accounts of events—that is, fiction and nonfiction. Every "show" has a commercial sponsor, whether it be an account of an actual battle or a war movie. With only the frame of, for example, a "made-for-TV movie" or the "NBC Nightly News" to indicate whether the scene of a bomb-devastated airport belongs to art or reality, the television public has unconsciously accepted Fish's definition of literature as "language around which we have drawn a frame." And the television network executives know intuitively what Hayden White argues theoretically: that the intelligibility of historical accounts depends upon the fictive form of their presentation, the form the age accepts as convincing (99). Fish and White are explaining what Picasso demonstrated in his collages early in the century: that frame and context determine what the public perceives as art. (For a video-literate consumer culture, all television shows seem to present a more or less equal degree of "reality.")

The New Journalism, practiced by such writers as Tom Wolfe, Hunter Thompson, and Gay Talese, represents a deliberate rejection of the traditional journalist's "objectivity" toward the subject matter in its embrace of literary conventions for journalistic purposes. Talese has said: "We want to pursue reporting as an art form. I think that is wonderful: the reporter as the artist" (Brady 110).

5. See the systems theorist Ervin Laszlo's *The Inner Limits of Mankind* (5–6) for a succinct discussion of the presuppositions of a capitalist society. Laszlo goes on to delineate values appropriate to "the global age," including the following:

—that the perennial wisdom of the great religions, of great artists and great humanists is needed to complement the technical expertise of the sciences because human beings and societies are, and always will be, far more than an assemblage of processes that can be reduced to scientifically determinable "facts";

—that we need to complement specialists, who know more and more about less and less, with highly trained generalists who know just enough about almost everything to be able to see the whole forest and not only a multiplicity of trees, and who can therefore be better relied upon to guide our steps through the many forks and crossroads along our way;

—that technology should be the servant, not the master of humanity, and its applications should be assessed in terms not merely of economic benefit, but of human, social and environmental benefit; . . .

—that ideas play a vital catalytic role in our world, and lie at the origin not merely of technological innovations but more importantly of those social and cultural advances so sorely needed to speed up mankind's adjustment to its new age. (16–18)

6. Holistic Practices

1. In *Literary Theory* Terry Eagleton writes:

Becoming certificated by the state as proficient in literary studies is a matter of being able to talk and write in certain ways. It is this which is being taught, examined and certificated, not what you personally think or believe, though what is thinkable will of course be constrained by the language itself. You can think or believe what you want, as long as you can speak this particular language. Nobody is especially concerned about what you say, with what extreme, moderate, radical or conservative positions you adopt, provided that they are compatible with, and can be articulated within, a specific form of discourse. It is just that certain meanings and positions will not be articulable within it. Literary studies, in other words, are a question of the signifier, not of the signified. Those employed to teach you this form of discourse will remember whether or not you were able to speak it proficiently long after they have forgotten what you said. (201)

Works Cited

Angell, James Rowland. "The Influence of Darwin on Psychology." *Psychological Review* 16 (1909): 152–69.

Applebee, Arthur N. *Tradition and Reform in the Teaching of English: A History.* Urbana, Ill.: National Council of Teachers of English, 1974.

Aristotle. *The Poetics.* Trans. S. H. Butcher. *Aristotle's Theory of Poetry and Fine Art.* 1911. New York: Dover, 1951.

Arnold, Matthew. *The Complete Works of Matthew Arnold.* Ed. R. H. Super. Ann Arbor: U of Michigan P, 1968.

———. *Culture and Anarchy.* Ed. J. Dover Wilson. Cambridge: Cambridge UP, 1960.

Atkinson, William P. "Liberal Education of the Nineteenth Century." *Popular Science Monthly* 4 (1873): 1–26.

Babbitt, Irving. *Literature and the American College: Essays in Defense of the Humanities.* Boston: Houghton, Mifflin, 1908.

Bacon, Francis. *The Works of Francis Bacon.* Ed. James Spedding, Robert Leslie Ellis, and Douglas Denon Heath. 1870. New York: Garrett Press, 1968.

Baker, Houston A. *Blues, Ideology, and Afro-American Literature.* Chicago: University of Chicago P, 1984.

Balzac, Honoré de. *At the Sign of the Cat and Racket.* New York: Peter Fenelon and Son, 1900.

Barnard, F. A. P. "Science and Our Educational System." *Popular Science Monthly* 2 (1873): 695–98.

Barthelme, Donald. *Snow White.* 1965. New York: Atheneum, 1982.

Barthes, Roland. *Image-Music-Text.* Trans. Stephen Heath. New York: Hill and Wang, 1977.

———. *The Pleasure of the Text.* Trans. Richard Miller. New York: Hill and Wang, 1975.

Baym, Nina. "Melodramas of Beset Manhood: How Theories of American Fiction Exclude Women Authors." *The New Feminist Criticism: Essays on Women, Literature, and Theory.* Ed. Elaine Showalter. New York: Pantheon, 1985.

Bloland, Harland G., and Sue M. Bloland. *American Learned Societies in Transition: The Impact of Dissent and Recession*. New York: McGraw-Hill, 1974.

Boller, Paul F., Jr. *American Thought in Transition: The Impact of Evolutionary Naturalism, 1865–1900*. Chicago: Rand McNally, 1969.

Bradley, A. C. *Oxford Lectures on Poetry*. London: Macmillan, 1934.

Brady, John. "Gay Talese: An Interview." Ed. Ronald Weber. New York: Hastings House, 1974.

Breton, André. *Manifestoes of Surrealism*. Trans. Richard Seaver and Helen R. Lane. Ann Arbor: U of Michigan P, 1972.

Brooks, Cleanth. *The Well-Wrought Urn*. New York: Harcourt, Brace and World, 1947.

Brooks, Cleanth, and Robert Penn Warren. *Understanding Poetry*. New York: Henry Holt, 1938.

Cain, William. *The Crisis in Criticism: Theory, Literature, and Reform in English Studies*. Baltimore: Johns Hopkins UP, 1984.

Calvino, Italo. *Invisible Cities*. Trans. William Weaver. New York: Harcourt Brace Jovanovich, 1974.

Cantarow, Ellen. "Why Teach Literature? An Account of How I Came to Ask That Question." *The Politics of Literature*. Ed. Louis Kampf and Paul Lauter. New York: Pantheon, 1970.

Capra, Fritjof. *The Turning Point: Science, Society, and the Rising Culture*. New York: Bantam, 1982.

Chambers, Robert. *Vestiges of the Natural History of Creation*. New York: Humanities Press, 1969.

Chipp, Herschel B., ed. *Theories of Modern Art: A Source Book by Artists and Critics*. Berkeley: U of California P, 1968.

Clay, Jean, ed. *Impressionism*. Secaucus: Chartwell Books, 1973.

Coleridge, Samuel Taylor. *Biographia Literaria*. Ed. James Engell and W. Jackson Bate. Vol. 2 of *The Collected Works of Samuel Taylor Coleridge*. Princeton: Princeton UP, 1983.

Cooke, Josiah Parsons. "The Greek Question." *Popular Science Monthly* 24 (1883): 1–6.

Corson, Hiram. *The Aims of Literary Study*. New York: Macmillan, 1910.

Coover, Robert. *Pricksongs and Descants*. New York: New American Library, 1970.

Craige, Betty Jean. *Literary Relativity: An Essay on Twentieth-Century Narrative*. Lewisburg: Bucknell UP, 1982.

Cronyn, George W. *The Path on the Rainbow: An Anthology of Songs and Chants from the Indians of North America*. New York: Boni and Liveright, 1918.

Culler, Jonathan. *On Deconstruction*. Ithaca: Cornell UP, 1982.

———. *The Pursuit of Signs*. Ithaca: Cornell UP, 1981.

Darwin, Charles. *The Descent of Man, and Selection in Relation to Sex*. Princeton: Princeton UP, 1981.

————. *The Origin of Species*. Intro. Sir Julian Huxley. New York: New American Library, 1958.

Derrida, Jacques. "Structure, Sign, and Play in the Discourse of the Human Sciences." *The Structuralist Controversy: The Languages of Criticism and the Sciences of Man*. Ed. Richard Macksey and Eugenio Donato. Baltimore: Johns Hopkins UP, 1972.

Descartes, René. *Philosophical Writings*. Trans. Elizabeth Anscombe and Peter Thomas Geach. Ed. Elizabeth Anscombe and Peter Thomas Geach. Intro. Alexandre Koyre. London: Thomas Nelson and Sons, 1954.

Dewey, John. "Academic Freedom." *Educational Review* 23 (1902): 1–14.

————. *The Influence of Darwin on Philosophy*. 1910. Bloomington: Indiana UP, 1965.

————. *Reconstruction in Philosophy*. New York: Henry Holt, 1920.

Dolbear, A. E. "Metamorphoses in Education." *Popular Science Monthly* 39 (1891): 750–61.

Draper, Andrew S. "The American Type of University." *Science* 26 (1907): 33–43.

Dyer, Thomas G. *The University of Georgia: A Bicentennial History, 1785–1985*. Athens: U of Georgia P, 1985.

Eagleton, Terry. *Literary Theory: An Introduction*. Minneapolis: U of Minnesota P, 1983.

Eliot, C. W. *Charles W. Eliot: The Man and His Beliefs*. Vol. 1. Ed. William Allan Neilson. New York: Harper and Brothers, 1926.

Eliot, T. S. *The Sacred Wood: Essays on Poetry and Criticism*. 3rd ed. London: Methuen, 1932.

Ellis, Katherine. "Arnold's Other Axiom." *The Politics of Literature*. Ed. Louis Kampf and Paul Lauter. New York: Pantheon, 1970.

Fellman, David. "Academic Freedom." *Dictionary of the History of Ideas: Studies of Selected Pivotal Ideas*. Ed. Philip P. Wiener. New York: Charles Scribner's Sons, 1968.

Ferguson, Marilyn. *The Aquarian Conspiracy: Personal and Social Transformation in the 1980s*. Los Angeles: Tarcher, 1980.

Fiedler, Leslie. "Cross the Border—Close That Gap: Post-Modernism." *Postmodernism in American Literature: A Critical Anthology*. Ed. Manfred Putz and Peter Freese. Darmstadt: Thesen Verlag, 1984.

————. *What Was Literature? Culture and Mass Society*. New York: Simon and Schuster, 1982.

Fish, Stanley. *Is There a Text in This Class? The Authority of Interpretive Communities*. Cambridge: Harvard UP, 1980.

Foucart, Bruno. *Courbet*. Trans. Alice Sachs. New York: Crown, 1977.

Foucault, Michel. *Language, Counter-Memory, Practice: Selected Essays and Interviews*. Ed. Donald F. Bouchard. Trans. Donald F. Bouchard and Sherry Simon. Ithaca: Cornell UP, 1977.

Franklin, Bruce. "English as an Institution: The Role of Class." *English Literature: Opening Up the Canon*. Ed. Leslie Fiedler and Houston Baker. Baltimore: Johns Hopkins UP, 1981.

_____. "The Teaching of Literature in the Highest Academies of the Empire." *The Politics of Literature*. Ed. Louis Kampf and Paul Lauter. New York: Pantheon, 1970.

Franklin, Phyllis. "English Studies: The World of Scholarship in 1883." *PMLA* 99 (1984): 356–70.

Freud, Sigmund. *The Standard Edition of the Complete Psychological Works of Sigmund Freud*. Ed. James Strachey, in collaboration with Anna Freud. London: Hogarth, 1959.

Gerard, Alexander. *An Essay on Genius*. 1774. Ed. Bernhard Fabian. Munich: Wilhelm Fink Verlag, 1966.

Giamatti, A. Bartlett. *The University and the Public Interest*. New York: Atheneum, 1981.

Gilman, Daniel Coit. *University Problems in the United States*. New York: Century, 1898.

Golding, Alan C. "A History of American Poetry Anthologies." *Canons*. Ed. Robert von Hallberg. Chicago: U of Chicago P, 1983.

Gould, Stephen Jay. "Darwinism Defined: The Difference Between Fact and Theory." *Discover* 8.1 (1987): 64–70.

_____. *The Mismeasure of Man*. New York: Norton, 1981.

Graff, Gerald. *Professing Literature: An Institutional History*. Chicago: U of Chicago P, 1987.

Hartman, Geoffrey H. *Criticism in the Wilderness*. New Haven: Yale UP, 1980.

_____. "Preface." *Deconstruction and Criticism*. Ed. Harold Bloom, Paul de Man, Jacques Derrida, Geoffrey Hartman, and J. Hillis Miller. New York: Seabury Press, 1979.

Hassan, Ihab. *Paracriticisms: Seven Speculations of the Times*. Urbana: U of Illinois P, 1975.

_____. "The Re-Vision of Literature: Rhetoric, Imagination, Vision." *Postmodernism in American Literature: A Critical Anthology*. Ed. Manfred Putz and Peter Freese. Darmstadt: Thesen-Verlag, 1984.

Heilbrun, Carolyn G. "The Profession and Society, 1958–83." *PMLA* 99 (1984): 408–13.

Heisenberg, Werner. *The Physicist's Conception of Nature*. Trans. Arnold J. Pomerans. New York: Harcourt, Brace and World, 1958.

Works Cited   149

Hofstadter, Richard. *The Development of Higher Education in America*. Richard Hofstadter and C. DeWitt Hardy, *The Development and Scope of Higher Education in the United States*. New York: Columbia UP, 1952.

Honan, Park. *Matthew Arnold: A Life*. Cambridge: Harvard UP, 1983.

Hughes, Thomas Parke. *Changing Attitudes Toward American Technology*. New York: Harper and Row, 1975.

Huxley, Thomas H. *Science and Education: Essays*. New York: D. Appleton, 1900.

Jarry, Alfred. *King Ubu. Modern French Theatre: An Anthology of Plays*. Trans. and ed. Michael Benedikt and George E. Wellwarth. New York: Dutton, 1966.

Kampf, Louis, and Paul Lauter, eds. *The Politics of Literature*. New York: Pantheon, 1970.

Kant, Immanuel. *Kant's Critique of Judgement*. Trans. J. H. Bernard. 2nd ed. London: Macmillan, 1931.

Keller, Evelyn Fox. *Reflections on Gender and Science*. New Haven: Yale UP, 1985.

Kelly, Robert Lincoln. *The American Colleges and the Social Order*. New York: Macmillan, 1940.

Kerr, Clark. *The Uses of the University*. Cambridge: Harvard UP, 1963.

Kibel, Alvin C. "The Canonical Text." *Reading in the 1980s*. Ed. Stephen Graubard. New York: R. R. Bowker, 1983.

Kristeller, Paul Oskar. "The Modern System of the Arts: A Study in the History of Aesthetics (I)." *Journal of the History of Ideas* 12.4 (1951): 496–527.

———. "The Modern System of the Arts: A Study in the History of Aesthetics (II)." *Journal of the History of Ideas* 13.1 (1952): 17–46.

Krupat, Arnold. "Native American Literature and the Canon." *Canons*. Ed. Robert von Hallberg. Chicago: U of Chicago P, 1983.

Kuhn, Thomas S. *The Structure of Scientific Revolutions*. 2nd ed. Chicago: U of Chicago P, 1970.

Laszlo, Ervin. *The Inner Limits of Mankind: Heretical Reflections on Today's Values, Culture and Politics*. Oxford: Pergamon Press, 1978.

Leavis. F. R. *Nor Shall My Sword: Discourses on Pluralism, Compassion and Social Hope*. New York: Barnes and Noble, 1972.

Macksey, Richard, and Eugenio Donato. *The Structuralist Controversy: The Languages of Criticism and the Sciences of Man*. Baltimore: Johns Hopkins UP, 1972. Originally published as *The Languages of Criticism and the Sciences of Man*, 1970.

MacLeish, Archibald. "The Irresponsibles." *The Nation* 150 (1940): 618–23.

McLuhan, Marshall. *The Gutenberg Galaxy: The Making of Typographic Man*. Toronto: U of Toronto P, 1962.

———. *The Medium Is the Massage: An Inventory of Effects*. New York: Bantam, 1967.

———. *Understanding Media: The Extensions of Man*. 2nd ed. New York: New American Library, 1964.

Meese, Elizabeth A. "Archival Materials: The Problem of Literary Reputation." *Women in Print I*. Ed. Joan E. Hartman and Ellen Messer-Davidow. New York: Modern Language Association, 1982.

Merchant, Carolyn. *The Death of Nature: Women, Ecology and the Scientific Revolution*. San Francisco: Harper and Row, 1980.

Metzger, Walter P. *The Age of the University*. Richard Hofstadter and Walter P. Metzger, *The Development of Academic Freedom in the United States*. New York: Columbia UP, 1955.

Mill, John Stuart. *Mill's Essays on Literature and Society*. Ed. J. B. Schneewind. New York: Collier Books, 1965.

Miller, J. Hillis. "The Critic as Host." *Deconstruction and Criticism*. Ed. Harold Bloom, Paul de Man, Jacques Derrida, Geoffrey Hartman, and J. Hillis Miller. New York: Seabury Press, 1979.

Milton, John. *Complete Prose Works of John Milton*. Vol. 2: *1643–1648*. New Haven: Yale UP, 1959.

Monroe, Harriet and Alice Corbin Henderson, eds. *The New Poetry: An Anthology of Twentieth-Century Verse in English*. New York: MacMillan, 1932.

Mozley, J. B. "Modern Literatures in the Higher Education." *Popular Science Monthly* 1 (1872): 396–405.

Naisbitt, John. *Megatrends: Ten New Directions Transforming Lives*. New York: Warner, 1982.

Newman, John Henry Cardinal. *The Idea of a University*. Ed. Martin J. Svaglic. Notre Dame: U of Notre Dame P, 1982.

Nietzsche, Friedrich. *The Gay Science*. Trans. Walter Kaufmann. New York: Random House, 1974.

Odum, Eugene P. "The Attitude Revolution." *The Crisis of Survival*. Glenview: Scott, Foresman, 1970.

———. "Diversity and the Emergence of Integrative Disciplines in Universities." *Southern University Conference 1978*. Birmingham: Birmingham-Southern College, 1978. 9–13.

———. "The Emergence of Ecology as a New Integrative Discipline." *Science* 195 (1977): 1289–93.

Ohmann, Richard. *English in America: A Radical View of the Profession*. New York: Oxford UP, 1976.

———. "Teaching and Studying Literature at the End of Ideology." *The Politics of Literature*. Ed. Louis Kampf and Paul Lauter. New York: Pantheon, 1970.

Ong, Walter J. *Orality and Literacy: The Technologizing of the Word*. London: Methuen, 1982.

Parker, William Riley. "The MLA, 1883–1953." *PMLA* 68 (1953): 3–39.

———. "Where Do English Departments Come From?" *College English* 28 (1967): 339–51.

Pascal, Blaise. *Pensees et opuscules.* Ed. Leon Brunschvicg. Paris: Classiques Hachette, 1908–25.

————. *Pensees: Notes on Religion and Other Subjects.* Ed. Louis Lafuma. Trans. John Warrington. London: J. M. Dent and Sons, 1960.

Peacock, Thomas Love. "The Four Ages of Poetry." *A Defence of Poetry / The Four Ages of Poetry.* Ed. John E. Jordan. Indianapolis: Bobbs-Merrill, 1965.

Phillips, D. E. "The Elective System in American Education." *Pedagogical Seminary* 8 (1901): 206–30.

Pizer, Donald. "The Evolutionary Foundation of W. D. Howells's *Criticism and Fiction.*" *Philological Quarterly* 40 (1961): 91–103.

————. *Realism and Naturalism in Nineteenth-Century American Literature.* New York: Russell and Russell, 1976.

Porter, Noah. *The American Colleges and the American Public.* New Haven: Charles C. Chatfield, 1870.

Ransom, John Crowe. *The New Criticism.* Norfolk: New Directions, 1941.

————. *The World's Body.* New York: Charles Scribner's Sons, 1938.

Robinson, Lillian S. "Who's Afraid of a Room of One's Own?" *The Politics of Literature.* Ed. Louis Kampf and Paul Lauter. New York: Pantheon, 1970.

Ross, Earle D. *Democracy's College.* Ames: Iowa State College P, 1942.

Rossi, Paolo. "Baconianism." *Dictionary of the History of Ideas: Studies of Selected Pivotal Ideas.* Ed. Philip P. Wiener. New York: Charles Scribner's Sons, 1968.

Ruse, Michael. *The Darwinian Revolution.* Chicago: U of Chicago P, 1979.

Sartre, Jean-Paul. "Existentialism." Trans. Bernard Frechtman. *Existentialism and Human Emotions.* New York: Philosophical Library, 1957.

Saussure, Ferdinand de. *Course in General Linguistics: Ferdinand de Saussure.* Ed. Charles Bally and Albert Sechehaye, in collaboration with Albert Riedlinger. Trans. Wade Baskin. New York: McGraw-Hill, 1966.

Schmidt, George P. *The Liberal Arts College: A Chapter in American Cultural History.* New Brunswick: Rutgers UP, 1957.

Schurman, Jacob Gould. *The Ethical Import of Darwinism.* New York: Charles Scribner's Sons, 1893.

Shakespeare, William. *Hamlet. The Complete Works of William Shakespeare.* Ed. W. J. Craig. London: Oxford UP, 1964.

Shelley, Percy Bysshe. "A Defence of Poetry." *A Defence of Poetry / The Four Ages of Poetry.* Ed. John E. Jordan. Indianapolis: Bobbs-Merrill, 1965.

Shils, Edward. "The Order of Learning in the United States: The Ascendancy of the University." *The Organization of Knowledge in Modern America, 1860–1920.* Ed. Alexandra Oleson and John Voss. Baltimore: Johns Hopkins UP, 1979.

Shipman, Paul R. "The Classics That Educate Us." *Popular Science Monthly* 17 (1880): 145–55.

Sidney, Sir Philip. *Sir Philip Sidney's Defense of Poetry*. Ed. Lewis Soens. Lincoln: U of Nebraska P, 1970.

Small, Albion W. "Academic Freedom." *The Arena* 22 (1899): 463–72.

Smith, Barbara. "Toward a Black Feminist Criticism." *The New Feminist Criticism*. Ed. Elaine Showalter. New York: Pantheon, 1985.

Snow, C. P. *The Two Cultures and A Second Look: An Expanded Version of the Two Cultures and the Scientific Revolution*. Cambridge: Cambridge UP, 1965.

Solzhenitsyn, Alexander. *One Day in the Life of Ivan Denisovich*. Trans. Max Hayward and Ronald Hingley. New York: Bantam, 1963.

Sommers, Joseph. "Critical Approaches to Chicano Literature." *The Identification and Analysis of Chicano Literature*. Ed. Francisco Jimenez. New York: Bilingual Press/Editorial Bilingüe, 1979.

Sontag, Susan. *Against Interpretation*. New York: Dell, 1966.

Spariosu, Mihai. "Mimesis and Contemporary French Theory." *Mimesis in Contemporary Theory: An Interdisciplinary Approach*. Ed. Mihai Spariosu. Vol. 1. Amsterdam: John Benjamins, 1984.

Stein, Gertrude. *Writings and Lectures: 1909–1945*. Ed. Patricia Meyerowitz. Baltimore: Penguin, 1967.

Stevens, Wallace. *Opus Posthumous*. Ed. Samuel French Morse. New York: Knopf, 1975.

Taine, Hippolyte. "Introduction to *History of English Literature*." Trans. Henry van Laun. 1871. *Critical Theory Since Plato*. Ed. Hazard Adams. New York: Harcourt Brace Jovanovich, 1971.

Tate, Allen. *On the Limits of Poetry: Selected Essays, 1928–1948*. New York: Swallow Press and William Morrow, 1948.

Toffler, Alvin. *Previews and Premises*. New York: William Morrow, 1983.

———. *The Third Wave*. Toronto: Bantam, 1980.

Tompkins, Jane P. "Sentimental Power: *Uncle Tom's Cabin* and the Politics of Literary History." *The New Feminist Criticism: Essays on Women, Literature, and Theory*. Ed. Elaine Showalter. New York: Pantheon, 1985.

Untermeyer, Louis, ed. *American Poetry: From the Beginning to Whitman*. New York: Harcourt, Brace, 1931.

———. *Modern American Poetry: A Critical Anthology*. 4th ed. New York: Harcourt, Brace, 1930.

Veblen, Thorstein. *The Higher Learning in America*. New York: B. W. Huebsch, 1918.

Veysey, Laurence R. *The Emergence of the American University*. Chicago: U of Chicago P, 1970.

Warren, Robert Penn. Introduction. *Fifty Years of American Poetry*. New York: Abrams, 1984.

Wellek, René. "Realism in Literature." *Dictionary of the History of Ideas: Studies of*

Selected Pivotal Ideas. Ed. Philip P. Wiener. New York: Charles Scribner's Sons, 1968.

Wellek, René, and Austin Warren. *Theory of Literature*. 3rd ed. New York: Harcourt, Brace and World, 1970.

White, Hayden. *Tropics of Discourse: Essays in Cultural Criticism*. Baltimore: Johns Hopkins UP, 1978.

Whorf, Benjamin Lee. *Language, Thought, and Reality: Selected Writings of Benjamin Lee Whorf*. Ed. John B. Carroll. Cambridge: Massachusetts Institute of Technology P, 1956.

Williams, Raymond. *Marxism and Literature*. Oxford: Oxford UP, 1977.

Wilson, R. J. *Darwinism and the American Intellectual: A Book of Readings*. Homewood: The Dorsey Press, 1967.

Wimsatt, William, Jr. *The Verbal Icon: Studies in the Meaning of Poetry*. Lexington: U of Kentucky P, 1954.

Wofsy, Leon. "Biotechnology and the University." *Journal of Higher Education* 57 (1986): 477–92.

Wolfe, Tom. *The New Journalism*. New York: Harper and Row, 1973.

Woolf, Virginia. *A Room of One's Own*. New York: Harcourt, Brace and World, 1929.

Wordsworth, William. *Lyrical Ballads*. Ed. R. L. Brett and A. R. Jones. London: Methuen, 1965.

Wright, Chauncey. *Philosophical Discussions*. Ed. Charles Eliot Norton. New York: Henry Holt, 1877.

Youmans, Edward Livingston. "The Place of Science in the Higher Education." *Popular Science Monthly* 1 (1872): 624–27.

Young, Edward. *The Complete Works: Poetry and Prose*. Vol. II. Ed. James Nichols. 1854. Hildesheim: Georg Olms, 1968.

Young, Robert M. *Darwin's Metaphor: Nature's Place in Victorian Culture*. Cambridge: Cambridge UP, 1985.

Zola, Emile. "From *The Experimental Novel*." Trans. B. M. Sherman. 1893. *Critical Theory Since Plato*. Ed. Hazard Adams. New York: Harcourt Brace Jovanovich, 1971.PG